**This book is to be returned on or before
the last date stamped below.**

- 4 DEC 1996

28.01.98

Life & Work
in 19th Century
Britain

Rachel Hamer

Heinemann

Heinemann Library,
a division of Heinemann Publishers (Oxford) Ltd,
Halley Court, Jordan Hill, Oxford OX2 8EJ

OXFORD LONDON EDINBURGH MADRID
ATHENS BOLOGNA PARIS MELBOURNE
SYDNEY AUCKLAND SINGAPORE TOKYO
IBADAN NAIROBI HARARE GABORONE
PORTSMOUTH NH (USA)

First published 1995

95 96 97 98 10 9 8 7 6 5 4 3 2 1

**British Library Cataloguing Data is available
from the British Library on request.**

ISBN 0 431 07070 9

Designed by Ron Kamen, Green Door Design Ltd,
Basingstoke

Illustrated by Brian Kemp and Wayne Summers

Printed in Spain by Mateu Cromo

The front cover shows people waiting for help in the
workhouse in a painting by Sir Luke Fildes (1874).

Acknowledgements

The author and publisher would like to thank the
following for permission to reproduce photographs:

Bridgeman Art Gallery/Royal Holloway and Bedford
New College: Cover
Elton Collection, Ironbridge Gorge Museum Trust:
4.1
Mary Evans Picture Library: 1.2, 2.12, 3.1, 3.2, 3.4,
3.7, 4.3, 4.4, 5.1
Her Majesty the Queen: 4.9
Hulton Deutsch Collection: 4.5
Ipswich Borough Museums and Galleries: 1.1
Lawrence and Wishart: map on page 14
Mansell Collection: 2.4, 2.7, 2.8, 2.9, 2.13, 3.3
Master and Fellows of Trinity College, Cambridge:
4.6
Sunderland Public Libraries, Museum and Art
Gallery: Page 19

Every effort has been made to contact copyright
holders of material published in this book. Any
omissions will be rectified in subsequent printings if
notice is given to the publisher.

Details of written sources

In some sources the wording or sentence structure
has been simplified to ensure that the source is
accessible.

G. Best, *Mid-Victorian Britain, 1851-75*, Weidenfeld
and Nicolson, 1971: 5.4
William Cobbett, *Rural Rides*, Penguin, 1967: 2.6, 2.12
C. Culpin, *Making Modern Britain*, Collins
Educational, 1987: 5.3
Frank Victor Dawes, *Not in front of the servants*,
Century Hutchinson, 1989: 4.6
M.W. Flinn (ed.), *A Report on the Sanitary Conditions
of the Labouring Class of Great Britain, 1842*,
Edinburgh University Press, 1965: 2.12
Henry Mayhew, *London Labour and the London Poor,
1851*, Spring Books: 1.2, 4.7, 4.8
Peter Lane, *Batsford History Kits*, Batsford, 1975: 2.11
Peter and Mary Speed, *Working with Evidence: The
Industrial Revolution*, Oxford University Press, 1985:
2.14
G.M. Young, *Victorian Essays*, Oxford University
Press, 1962: 4.2

> **Note**
>
> In this book some of the words are printed in **bold**
> type. This indicates that the word is listed in the
> glossary on page 31. The glossary gives a brief
> explanation of words that may be new to you.

Contents

Unit 1   Changes in Britain 1750-1900: An Overview   4

Unit 2   What were the effects of the Industrial Revolution?   6

Unit 3   How did reform come about?   14

Unit 4   What were living standards like in
the second half of the 19th century?   22

Unit 5   Was Britain a better place to live in 1900 than in 1750?   28

Glossary   31

Index   32

Changes in Britain 1750–1900: An Overview

In 1750 most people in Britain lived in small villages. London, with a population of 500,000 people, was the only city of any size. The majority of people earned their living by farming in ways which had hardly changed since the Middle Ages.

There were few **factories**. Almost all the industries were on a small scale. Coal mines employed only a few miners and iron was smelted in clearings in the forests. The making of woollen cloth was the most important industry. This was usually carried out in people's homes with all the family joining in. This was known as the domestic system.

Between 1750 and 1900 the population of Britain grew very quickly. From eight million in 1750 it increased to 21 million in 1851. By 1900 it was 37 million.

This increase in population sparked off an increased demand for goods. British industry became based in large mechanized factories which were built on the coal fields. The machines were driven by steam engines. Around the factories grew large towns, as people moved from the countryside in search of work.

By 1851, Britain was the **'workshop of the world'**. The Great Exhibition was opened by Queen Victoria. It was held to celebrate the 'Works of Industry of All Nations' in the specially

1750

8 out of every 10 people lived in the country

1850

5 out of every 10 people lived in the country

In 1850 a larger proportion of people lived in the towns compared with 1750.

SOURCE *1*

The Suffolk village of East Bergholt painted by John Constable (1776–1837) in about 1812. Constable was a landscape painter. He lived for a time in East Bergholt.

SOURCE 2

'Under the Viaduct', an engraving of London, completed in 1872, by the French artist Gustave Doré (1833–83).

	1800	1900
Birmingham	71	760
Bradford	13	280
Liverpool	82	700
Manchester	75	645

Population growth in some British cities 1800 – 1900 (figures in thousands).

SOURCE 3

The people press, two and three deep, watching intently the operations of the moving machinery. Farmers with their mouths wide agape, lean over the bars to see the self-acting mules at work. They smile as they see the frame automatically draw itself out and run back in again.

Henry Mayhew, a social commentator and journalist, describing the interest in machinery at the Great Exhibition of 1851.

PAXTON

Joseph Paxton (1801–1865) was the son of a farmer. He became the head gardener at Chatsworth House in Derbyshire. Here he grew exotic flowers, made water gardens and built a huge conservatory for growing rare plants. It was this that gave him the inspired idea to design the Crystal Palace for the Great Exhibition in 1851.

built Crystal Palace. Here, the six million people who came to the building in Hyde Park could see goods which were traded in all parts of the world.

The greatest inventions of the age were British. Britain produced more than half the world's cotton cloth. Iron foundries poured out more than half the world's pig iron. Britain had the largest merchant fleet which carried goods to the **British Empire** and the rest of the world.

For many people the changes were bewildering. The old certainties of village life began to disappear. The rapidly growing towns were never big enough to accommodate the numbers scrambling for house room. They were therefore overcrowded and lacked sanitation. In the face of a rising population, with the factories acting like magnets for those who needed jobs, the towns became dreadful places. Disease was always frightening and many people lived in squalid houses.

This book is about how these changes – often referred to as the **Industrial Revolution** – affected the living and working conditions of the people.

What were the effects of the Industrial Revolution?

Working in the first factories

The cotton industry was the first to become factory-based. The first modern factory was founded in 1771 by Richard Arkwright at Cromford in Derbyshire. Here, the machines were powered by water. In 1780 Arkwright built the first cotton mill (factory) to be powered by a steam engine. Arkwright made large profits and other people soon followed his example. Edward Baines, writing in 1825 about Oldham in Lancashire, noted: 'Sixty years ago there was not a cotton mill in these parts; at present there are no fewer than 65.'

Factory discipline

The early factories were often dangerous, unhealthy and miserable places. The whole system was new, untried and unregulated. Working conditions varied greatly and improvements came only after many working people had experienced years of hardship and distress. Going 'out to work' was a completely new way of life. For factory owners it meant finding ways of organizing large numbers of people and making a profit. For employees it meant keeping to time and going out to work every weekday, instead of being at home. It also meant that for the first time the family was split up. Many factories had strict rules; those who broke them were punished. Workers were often heavily fined and the threat of dismissal was real. Both children and adults were beaten for making mistakes or falling asleep.

SOURCE 1

Area	1787	1835
Cheshire	8	109
Derbys	22	96
Lancs	41	683
Yorks	11	126
Scotland	19	159

The number of cotton factories in selected areas of Britain, 1787 and 1835.

SOURCE 2

NOTICE
List of Fines

For opening a window 1/-
For being dirty at work 1/-
For leaving an oil can out of place 1/-
For being five minutes after the bell 1/-
For having waste on the spindles 1/-
For whistling at work 1/-

A list of fines in a Manchester factory, 1840.

SOURCE 3

When my father introduced machinery into his own mill, the hours of labour were increased to twelve, for five days in the week, and eleven for Saturdays, making seventy one hours in the week. Other mill-owners, who used the same sort of machinery, worked their hands as much as eighty four hours a week.

John Fielden, a factory owner from Todmorden, Yorkshire, describing the long hours worked in the early factories.

SOURCE 4

Children in a spinning factory, 1830. Child labour was not new. It had been used under the domestic system. What was new was the dangerous machinery. Children swept under the unguarded machines whilst they were still in motion.

SOURCE 5

The task first given to him was to pick up the loose cotton that fell on the floor. He set to with diligence, although much terrified by the whirling motion and noise of the machinery, and half suffocated by the dust. Unused to the stench, he soon felt sick and his back ached with the constant bending. Blincoe, therefore, sat down. His task-master, Smith, told him that he must keep on his legs. He did so till twelve o' clock, being six and an half hours without rest. The moment the bell rang for dinner everyone rushed to get out of the mill as quickly as possible.

*A description of Robert Blincoe's first day working in a cotton mill. It is taken from **A memoir of Robert Blincoe**, written by John Brown in 1828. Blincoe was seven years old.*

SOURCE 6

In this room, which is lit from above, and in the most convenient and beautiful manner, there were 500 pairs of looms at work and 50 persons attending them. All the workers looked healthy and well dressed.

*From William Cobbett, **Rural Rides**, 1830. This book was an account of a tour around England. Cobbett was a Radical – he wanted working-class people to have the vote. Here, he is describing John Fielden's factory.*

Titus Salt

Not all factory owners treated their workers harshly. One business that really attracted the public eye was the great mill at Saltaire on the river Aire near Shipley, in Yorkshire, built by Sir Titus Salt. It was a model factory weaving mohair. Around the factory Salt built good quality housing for his workers. Sir Titus entertained 3,000 guests at a grand opening banquet, including over 2,000 workers brought by rail from his factory at Bradford. Such publicity and his prosperity helped to spread his ideas and encouraged others to follow his example. However, in a local paper *The Voice of the People*, he was nicknamed 'Tim Pepper' and mocked for his conceit in making his workers pay for a marble statue of himself.

SOURCE 7

Saltaire Mill in Yorkshire, a model weaving mill in the first model industrial town in Britain, founded in 1853 by Sir Titus Salt.

Living in the factory towns

Work in the factories began at 5.30 am. Everyone walked to work so they wanted to live as near to the factory as possible. Wages were low, so there was little money to spend on rent. It was essential to live as cheaply as possible. People moved into towns so rapidly and in such great numbers that there was not time to provide enough houses for them. Thousands of people were crowded into old or hastily built houses in the streets, or in closed courtyards near the factories.

Housing

For houses, as for factories, there were no laws to maintain standards. There were no effective safeguards to ensure a supply of clean water, proper drainage and sewerage, or to maintain the cleaning of the streets. The streets were not always paved. In the centre of the street was a gutter into which the dirty water from washing and cooking was poured. It often went stagnant and sometimes became clogged up with dead rats or rotting waste. The houses were grouped around a courtyard or in long terraces, often back to back. The **cesspit** was supposed to be emptied in buckets at night. When this was not done the sewage overflowed into the courtyard. Often the cesspit was next to the water pump which could cause contamination of the water. The smell was foul.

Close 75, High Street, Glasgow in 1868 – an example of overcrowded and insanitary conditions.

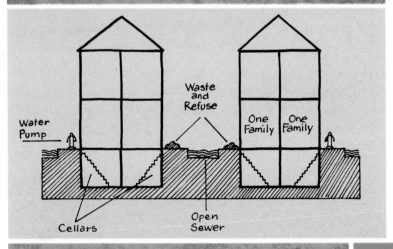

Back to back housing.

Cramped conditions

For most of the 19th century families could afford to rent only one room. The cheapest were cellars. They were usually very damp and had stone or earth floors. They had little light and were dark and cold. Rented rooms were generally not large enough for a whole family who had to cook, eat, wash and sleep in the limited space. There was a single grate for heat and cooking, with candles for light. In the summer it could be stifling as there was only one window and no through draught. Furniture was sparse. Living in this way, it was very difficult to keep clean and tidy. A few families, however, managed it (see Source 10).

The better-off lived in large houses on the outskirts of the town. They could afford to travel into the centre to work.

A Victorian family at home, living and dying in one room.

A poorer room, and yet a cleaner one I never saw; the table had been scoured until it shone again. There was a faded bit of carpeting on the floor and not a speck of dust from wall to wall. I have never seen a more striking instance of cleanliness taking away all the squalor of poverty.

Taken from an article in **The Bradford Chronicle** in 1849. Bradford was a large industrial city, which produced woollen cloth. Workers lived in terraced back to back houses.

THINK IT THROUGH

Look at Source 9. Think about all the difficulties of a family living in one room all the time. What would be hardest to put up with?

What does Source 12 tell us about Britain in the mid-19th century?

Diet

Cooking was very difficult. Bread was the staple food and was eaten with a scrape of butter or dripping or sometimes jam, with cups of tea for breakfast and tea. No plates or cooking utensils were needed for this, which made things easier. Boiled potatoes were the mainstay of dinner, with sometimes a little cheese, bacon or occasionally an egg. If there was meat on Sunday it was cooked in one pot with vegetables over the fire, or taken to a bakery to be cooked in an oven. There was little variety. Street sellers, such as piemen, sellers of hot green peas, eels, hot buns and puddings, helped to provide hot food if there was spare money to buy their wares.

Most families had to face disease. People accepted illness and early death as natural and normal. In the past there had been serious epidemics of plague or fever, but now that so many people were living together in one place infections such as cholera and typhus spread quickly and thousands of people died. The scale of such disasters was one reason which was, at last, to lead to improvements in public health and standards of building.

SOURCE 11

	Butter (1½lb)	7p
	Tea (1½oz)	2p
	Bacon (1½lb)	4p
	Milk (2 pints per day)	9p
	Meat (1lb on Sundays)	3p
	Potatoes	7p
	Sugar	4p
	Pepper, mustard and salt	1p
	Soap and candles	7½p
	Rent (per week)	17½p
	Total	**62p**

A week's budget for a family of seven in Manchester in 1833.

SOURCE 12

*The average age of death in 1842 in a town (Manchester) and a country area (Rutland). Taken from **A Report on the Sanitary Condition of the Labouring Class** by Edwin Chadwick (1800–90), a civil servant, who worked on the improvement of the **Poor Laws** and public health legislation. His report was published in 1842.*

	Gentry	Farmers/Traders	Labourers
Rutland	52	41	38
Manchester	38	20	17

Mining villages

Not all workers lived in towns and cities. Many lived in agricultural or industrial villages, like the mining villages in such areas as Northumberland, Durham, the Midlands and South Wales. These were close-knit communities, sharing in a common danger. The demand for coal increased rapidly. More and more coal was needed to power machines, for railways and later, steamships.

Pit work was hard and dangerous. Men, women and children were employed for up to twelve hours a day. **Hewers** dug out the coal, their work lit by three or four candles. The hurriers dragged the cut coal in small trucks. It was taken to the surface on hoists or carried in **corves** up ladders or steep passages. Small children, as young as five, were employed as trappers. As trucks came along their job was to open and close the wooden doors which were installed in the passage ways to ventilate the mine.

SOURCE **14**

Cause of death	Age		
	Under 13	13 – 18	Over 18
Fell down shaft	14	16	36
Drawn over pulley	3	–	3
Fall of stones or coal	15	14	72
Drowned	3	4	15
Explosion of gas	13	18	49
Suffocated	–	2	6
By tram waggons	4	5	12

The main causes of deaths in British coalmines, 1838.

SOURCE **13**

Colliers' cottages, 1844. Inside the floors were beaten earth. They were dimly lit. Many smelt of 'human impurities'.

There were many threats to health. Not only was there the danger of explosion or pit falls, but the air was heavy with floating coal dust and smelled foul from the gases found underground. Although the new steam pumps helped to reduce the water in the mines, flooding was still a problem.

Agricultural villages

Agricultural labourers still formed the largest single group of workers in the early 19th century. Apart from ploughmen, shepherds and waggoners, labourers had to do whatever jobs the season required. In general, wages were lower than those of factory workers or miners. Wages were also higher in the north of England than the south.

All the family worked when they could, to make a living wage for everyone. For example, the youngest children scared away crows; there were turnips to drag and clean and **gleaning** to be done after the harvest.

Even so, farm workers in many parts of England were very poor. Their **tied cottages** were often no more than a single room with a lean-to for animals and as damp and smelly as any factory worker's room. New machinery, especially the threshing machine, meant that fewer labourers were needed. The rising population made the situation worse. There was not enough work on the farms. There was also no longer a need for hand-woven woollen cloth which could supplement wages. In the north of England, this situation was helped by the existence of alternative work in the factories, mines and iron works. In southern England there was serious unemployment which led to the Swing Riots of 1830.

SOURCE 15

A young boy scaring crows. All the family needed to work to make a living wage.

SOURCE 16

Many labourers do not have jobs. Instead they are employed by the parish digging and breaking stones for the roads. Yesterday I saw three poor fellows digging stones, who told me that they never had anything but bread to eat, and water to wash it down. One of them was a widower with three children and his pay was eighteen pence per day. Just such was the state of things in France at the eve of the **French Revolution**.

*From **Rural Rides** by William Cobbett, 17 April 1830.*

DAVY

Humphry Davy (1778–1829) was a chemist and an inventor. He was an inspiring teacher and was constantly making experiments. After investigating firedamp (methane) he designed a safety lamp which made possible deeper and safer coal mining. The lamp saved the lives of a great many miners.

3

How did reform come about?

The reform of working conditions

For most working people, the Industrial Revolution meant long hours, low wages and poor housing. Sometimes **trade depressions** brought high unemployment and further hardship. To begin with nothing was done to help working people. Why did it take so long for the **reform** of working conditions to come about?

The Luddites

Without the right to vote or **combine** together, the only way for working people to make their discontent known was to present petitions or even turn to violence.

In 1811–12, many textile workers in Yorkshire, Lancashire, Nottinghamshire and Cheshire were thrown out of work by a trade depression. They blamed their plight on the introduction of machinery. Workers angrily smashed up machinery. These workers took their name from an invented character called Ned Ludd, and were known as Luddites.

The Swing Riots

In 1830 after a series of bad harvests, food prices went up. The farm labourers were also angry at the introduction of steam-driven threshing machines which threatened their jobs. Workers, led by a Captain Swing, an invented character, broke threshing machines and burnt haystacks.

The authorities were alarmed at these outbreaks of violence. They were afraid of a revolution taking place in England, like the one which had occurred in France in 1789. Instead of helping the workers, they punished them.

Early attempts to form trade unions

Some workers tried to help themselves by combining together. At first, these groups were called friendly societies and they helped fellow-workers to find jobs. They also gave out sick pay and funded funerals.

SOURCE 1

A cartoon from the time, portraying the Swing Riots. Do you think the cartoonist is sympathetic to the labourers?

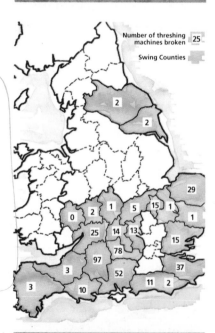

Counties in England where farm labourers rioted in 1830.

Attempts were made to form trades unions, which aimed to protect jobs, cut working hours and increase safety and wages.

In 1833, a number of unions joined together to form the Grand National Consolidated Trades Union (GNCTU). In 1834 six farm workers from the Dorset village of Tolpuddle were prosecuted for swearing an oath to form a local branch of the GNCTU. They were sentenced to transportation to Australia. Their harsh treatment put many workers off joining a union and the GNCTU collapsed.

What was needed was some direct link to Parliament where laws were made and could be changed.

Laissez-faire

Persuading Parliament that reforms were needed proved to be difficult. Why was this?

- Working people did not have the right to vote in the early 19th century.

- Most Members of Parliament were landowners and farmers from the south of England. They were not really interested in the problems of working people. Many had no knowledge of the northern textile mills.

- Most people believed that it was not the job of the government to interfere in people's lives; this belief was called *laissez-faire*.

The Ten Hours Movement

Two Factory Acts, passed in 1802 and 1819, were ineffective. In 1831 textile workers began campaigning for working hours to be limited to ten per day. There was a small number of MPs who were factory owners and supported shorter hours. They took up the cause. Michael Sadler, a linen manufacturer, became the leader of the Ten Hours Movement in Parliament. Most MPs, however, agreed with the argument that child labour and long hours were needed for the factories to make a profit.

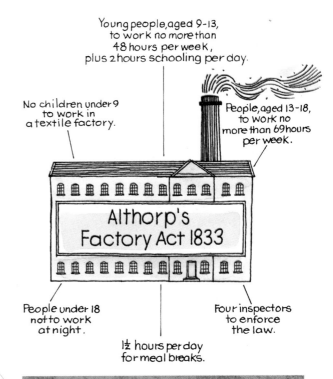

Young people, aged 9-13, to work no more than 48 hours per week, plus 2 hours schooling per day.

No children under 9 to work in a textile factory.

People, aged 13-18, to work no more than 69 hours per week.

Althorp's Factory Act 1833

People under 18 not to work at night.

1½ hours per day for meal breaks.

Four inspectors to enforce the law.

The terms of Althorp's Factory Act, 1833.

In 1832 the Earl of Shaftesbury became the leader of the Ten Hours Movement. He seemed to be an unlikely champion of the factory workers, as he came from a wealthy farming background. Shaftesbury, however, was a sincere and caring Christian. When he read reports in *The Times* about the conditions in factories, he was convinced that it was his duty to help. Parliament was pressured into setting up a commission to investigate conditions in the textile factories. The commission's report produced a mass of evidence which led to the passing of Althorp's Factory Act in 1833 (see above).

The 1833 Act did not alter conditions for many working men, women and children. It applied only to textile mills. Shaftesbury was disappointed that the Act had not achieved the ten hour day. It was important, however, because it was a first step towards the government accepting responsibility for decent working conditions. The belief in *laissez-faire* began to weaken.

The Collieries Act 1842

Shaftesbury continued the fight. In 1840 he persuaded the government to set up a Royal Commission to investigate conditions in the coal mines. Source 2 shows Shaftesbury visiting a mine as part of this campaign. The commission's report was published in 1842. It was graphically illustrated by artists who had been underground. The nation was shocked at the appalling conditions in which children and women worked. The Collieries Act of 1842 stopped boys under ten and women and girls from working underground in the mines. It also said that mining inspectors were to be appointed. Many women, however, were annoyed about the Act because it stopped them earning money.

Further legislation

Further factory acts followed (see page 17). In the last quarter of the 19th century half-day working on Saturdays and Bank Holidays began and inspectors checked all workplaces with machinery for manufacturing. Despite these improvements, there was still no insurance for workers. Unless workers belonged to a friendly society or a trade union, they received no money if they were absent from work.

(see page 17)

SOURCE 3

*Women coal bearers in Scotland, from the **Mines Report**, 1842.*

SOURCE 2

*Anthony Ashley Cooper (1801–85), 7th Earl of Shaftesbury visits a mine, taken from the **Mines Report**, 1842. The boy in the picture worked as a hurrier.*

FACTORY ACTS AFTER 1844

1844
Graham's Act

- No child under 8 years to work in a textile factory.
- A maximum 6½ hour day, with a half day at school for 8 – 13 year olds.
- Machinery to be guarded.

1847
Fielden's Ten Hours Act

- A maximum 10 hour day for women and children in textile factories. [Nothing said about the hours of men].

We can get round this!

Easy! We'll work a shift system with the children. The men will work all the time and we'll keep the machines running!

1850
Grey's Act

- Maximum working day for women and young people to be 10½ hours.
- Factories can be open only from 6.00 am to 6.00 pm.

Other laws passed

1867 All previous laws about textile factories to apply to all factories with more than 50 workers.

1874 Maximum week of 56½ hours for all factory workers.

1878 All workshops using machines to obey factory laws. Inspectors to check all factories and workshops.

Workers still not covered

Domestic servants

Seamstresses

Shopworkers

Farm labourers

COOPER

Although Anthony Ashley Cooper, Earl of Shaftesbury (1801–1885) was born into a rich and privileged family, his childhood was miserable. His parents were hard and cold. At school he witnessed a drunken pauper's funeral. He was shocked at the lack of respect and vowed to make the cause of the poor his own. Shaftesbury was also a strong evangelical Christian.

In 1826 Shaftesbury entered Parliament. He first campaigned to prevent the cruelty and neglect shown to lunatics. He then worked to improve the conditions in factories and mines. Shaftesbury also played a key role helping Edwin Chadwick to improve public health, campaigned to stop the use of climbing boys and supported Ragged Schools. Crowds lined the streets when he died to show their appreciation for his work.

The reform of living conditions

It proved even more difficult to get laws passed to improve the standard of housing and the water supply for the poor. The government was unwilling to do anything to improve matters. Besides, who was going to pay for the improvements? The local tax, or rate, was paid only by house owners. They lived in the better houses where there were better living conditions anyway. Why should they pay higher taxes to help others?

Progress came slowly. In 1835 the Municipal Corporations Act set up councils in all the main towns. Councils were given the powers, if they wished, to raise money for such things as paving the streets or putting in gas lights, but not much had been achieved.

Enter Edwin Chadwick

Chadwick's interest in people's health had grown when he was investigating the Poor Laws between 1832 and 1834. He thought that if he could show that foul living conditions caused disease, it would make the government realize that it cost less to prevent people getting ill than to pay to look after them when they could not work. In 1838 he got permission for a special survey of the conditions of the labouring classes in east London. The shocking findings of the report led to Chadwick's friend, the Bishop of London, proposing a report on all the cities in the country. *The Report on the Sanitary Condition of the Labouring Class* was completed in 1842 and became a best seller! It established that where there was no drainage, poor water supply and overcrowding there would be sickness and early death. This fact helped to challenge the views of many middle-class people that the way the poor lived was due to lack of effort on their part and that it was not the duty of the government to keep the people healthy. However, even a Royal Commission in 1844 confirming these findings still did not lead to real change.

The 1848 Public Health Act

Following an outbreak of cholera in 1848, Parliament passed the first Public Health Act. This set up a central Board of Health in London. The Act said that towns could set up their own local Board of Health if ten per cent of the ratepayers demanded it, or if the death rate was higher than 23 people per 1,000 in a year. The Act was not compulsory and many towns did not bother to follow it. The cholera outbreak passed away and interest in public health disappeared for a time.

Disease

The most feared disease was cholera, which first struck Britain in 1831. It caused the death of thousands. There were further serious outbreaks in 1848, 1854 and 1866. It was a terrible disease which resulted in fever, sickness and diarrhoea. Death usually followed. Although it mostly affected the overcrowded and insanitary tenements of the cities, middle-class families also suffered. Pressure for change began to grow as a result. In 1854 Dr John Snow carried out some research in Soho, London. He was able to prove that cholera was carried in contaminated water. Then, in 1865, Louis Pasteur, a French chemist, showed that germs caused decay; there was a firm connection between dirt and disease. People began to realize that towns would have to be cleaned up.

Power to the people

In 1867 the vote was given to all male householders in the towns. Until then only the upper-class males had been able to vote. Working-class people at last had a direct influence on Members of Parliament. Now MPs had to listen to those who lived in the cities.

The 1875 Public Health Act

Finally, in 1875, Parliament passed a Public Health Act which drew together previous Acts. It made all town councils build effective sewers and provide a clean water supply and a Medical Officer of Health to organize and inspect the work. This time the measures were compulsory.

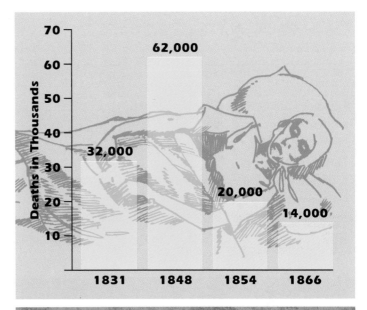

Deaths from cholera, 1831–66.

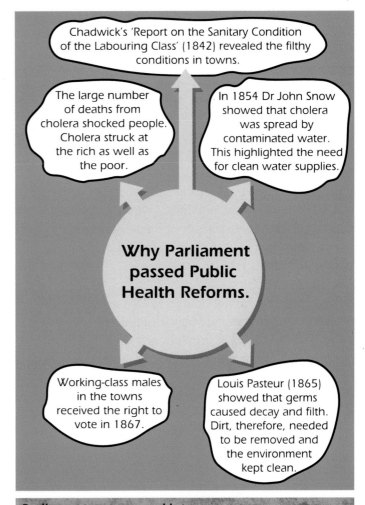

Parliament was pressed into passing Public Health Acts.

A row of terraced workers' houses built in the late 19th century. The problem was that not enough of these houses were built.

Improvements in housing – town councils

Parliament also introduced building regulations to improve the standard of housing. The Artisans' Dwelling Act (1875) gave town councils the power to knock down slums. They were also given the power to build new houses on the cleared ground or sell the land to private builders. Joseph Chamberlain, the lord mayor of Birmingham, took advantage of this Act and rebuilt the centre of the city. However, the Act was not a total success. Sometimes councils knocked down slums but did not build new houses to replace them. Private builders who built new houses on land bought from councils, usually charged such high rents that poorer people could not afford them.

Improvements in housing – private individuals

A number of individuals did important work to improve housing in the second half of the 19th century.

- In 1862 George Peabody, an American, gave a large sum of money for new workers' houses to be built in London.

- By 1871 Saltaire, built by Titus Salt (see page 8) had 800 houses, public baths, churches, shops and a park.

- Octavia Hill (1838–1912) borrowed money from rich friends and bought workers' houses to improve them. She then rented them out at a fair rent and still made a profit. She provided an example for other landlords to follow.

- In 1888 William Lever built Port Sunlight for his workers, and George Cadbury built the village of Bournville for his workers in 1895.

Despite these improvements, however, there were still many people living in cramped back to back houses.

Food and Drink

In the early 19th century factory workers were paid in tokens under the truck system. The only place the tokens could be spent was in the factory-owner's shop! The food here was often costly and had been tampered with (see Source 7). Favourite tricks in many shops were putting chalk in the flour and salt in the beer.

The Co-operative Movement

In 1844, a group of Rochdale weavers paid £1 each to open a shop in Toad Lane. Here they sold pure food at a fair price. If you bought goods at the shop you became a member and received a share of the profits (the dividend). The idea was so succesful that, by 1850, there were over 100 similar shops in the north of England. This was the start of the Co-operative Movement, which is still going today.

In 1871 a law was passed which made it illegal to pay workers in tokens. The Sale of Food and Drugs Act (1875) appointed shop inspectors to make sure that food was pure and shops clean.

'How food and drink were made!' – a cartoon from 1845, by George Cruikshank. What does it say about the production of food and drink?

HILL

Octavia Hill (1838–1912) came from a family with a tradition of caring. Her grandfather, Dr Southwood Smith, worked with Chadwick and Shaftesbury. From her grandfather she learnt about the conditions and homes of the poor. At the age of 14 she was teaching children in ragged schools.

When visiting London Octavia became convinced of the urgent need to improve housing. With the help and support of friends like John Ruskin she bought up slum properties and then improved them. She ran the properties on a proper business footing, and the rents paid for further improvements. Repairs were promptly dealt with and cleaning supervised.

Octavia advised the government on the Artisans' Dwellings Act (1875) and campaigned for open spaces for the public. She also helped to found the National Trust in 1894.

What were living standards like in the second half of the 19th century?

Despite Parliament passing legislation to improve housing, public health and working conditions, the standard of living still varied greatly.

Skilled workers

It seems that people with a regular and secure job adapted better to the rapid industrial changes which had been taking place. About one-tenth of the working population were skilled **artisans**. Their wages were twice those of a factory worker and their conditions of work much better. The key to their relatively favoured position was often a long **apprenticeship** when they learnt their skills. From 1851 many skilled workers were able to join a trade union, which fought to protect members' jobs, raise wages and improve working conditions. Printers, jewellers, instrument workers, engineers, shipwrights and carpenters were all organized into trade unions. Workers in the newer trades such as fine cotton spinners, calico printers and dyers could afford to rent better houses and own many comforts. Unskilled workers, however, did not have any trade unions to join.

SOURCE 1

A union membership certificate of the Amalgamated Society of Engineers, a trade union for skilled workers, formed in 1851.

SOURCE 2

We will take a printer, a skilled man in good employ – 58 hours a week and a half holiday on Saturday. He travels to work by horse-drawn bus, wearing a morning coat and tall hat. He takes his midday meal at a chop house – a plate of veal and ham and a pint of good beer, one shilling [5p]. The father has a vote. The children, you may be sure, go regularly to school; on Saturday afternoon the family take a steamer to Greenwich or Gravesend. Sunday morning they all go to church or chapel while the joint is cooking in the baker's shop and in the afternoon they walk in the park and have their friends to tea. Their annual fortnight will be spent at Margate, if they want to be jolly.

A description of late Victorian England by an historian, G. M. Young, who began his life in the last twenty years of Queen Victoria's reign.

SOURCE 3

The Salvation Army serving hot stew to the poor at the Conder Street Mission Hall, London, in 1881. Many people still had to rely on charity.

Unskilled workers

There were many sorts of labouring jobs in the ports and cities. These included dockers and dragmen, hodmen, builders, porters and coal backers. None of these jobs had any security. Workers were paid by the day or perhaps the week. In good years they might be employed for most of the year, but this might depend on their age, their health or even the weather. In times of depression work was hard to find; only the young and strong were likely to be hired.

In the 1880s trade unions for unskilled workers were formed. In 1889 the London dockers went on strike and won an increase in wages from the employers. Trade union membership began to rise.

For those ordinary families too poor to save it did not take much to bring disaster. There was very real fear of becoming ill for any length of time; or getting injured at work; losing a job or simply becoming too old and infirm to work any more. There was no National Insurance scheme and no old age pension. For many people there was no safety net other than the dreaded **workhouse**.

In the last years of the 19th century reports by Charles Booth in London and Seebohm Rowntree in York were published which provided evidence that, not only the elderly and those without work led miserable lives, but that many unskilled workers were paid such low wages that they could not afford the bare necessities of life. People like this probably numbered one-third of the population in these two cities. There was pressure for even more change after 1900.

Education

In the early 19th century schools for working-class children were provided by voluntary bodies. In 1870 Forster's Education Act introduced Board Schools for children aged 5–12. These schools were financed by the local rates and government grants; they provided a basic grounding in the **3Rs**. By 1899 elementary schooling to the age of 12 was free and compulsory. Pressure was growing for improved standards, and opportunities for secondary education were set out in the important Education Act of 1902.

THINK IT THROUGH

Why was educational opportunity so important to the working class?

The middle classes

The growing middle classes had far more security and lived much more comfortable lives. People in this section of society were identified by the 1841 **census** as

- independent persons (people with a private income).

- people in the professions (doctors, lawyers and teachers).

- government officers, people in the army, navy and civil service.

By the late 19th century the middle classes were more important than they had ever been before. They were defined by their greater income, which was expected to increase through life. However, within the middle class there was a big difference between the wealth of a successful factory owner and smaller merchants, shopkeepers or master tailors; between lawyers and clerks or schoolteachers. But they all described themselves as respectable people who did not earn their living by manual labour.

Middle-class housing in the late 19th century. Such detached houses were built on the edge of towns.

An upper middle-class Victorian living room.

Their income allowed them to rent or buy a comfortable home in a favourable area. For the lower middle class this might mean a terraced house with three bedrooms and three living rooms. Inside there was an increasing emphasis on comfort and decor. For those who could afford it, a kitchen, dining room, drawing room, library and three family bedrooms were desirable; plus a nursery and two servants' rooms.

Food was an important part of the budget. Entertaining for a well-off family was expensive. Many middle-class people travelled to work as they lived away from the town centre in the suburbs. Some owned carriages, but they were expensive to maintain. Most took a cab or, later, went to work by train. Clothes, too, were expensive as it was considered necessary to keep up with the fashion of the day.

Domestic servants

More than a million people at this time worked as domestic servants. In middle-class houses, except the very largest which had very large staffs, there would usually be three female servants. They would consist of a cook/housekeeper, a parlour maid and a 'tweeny' who did the rough work. Sometimes a manservant would be employed, perhaps to look after the horses or to act as butler and be in charge of the wine cellar. Even the least well-off people would employ one servant to come in each day.

For most of the year the servants' working day began before 6 am, when they lit the fires before breakfast, and ended when the warming pans had been put in the beds at night. No allowance was made if the servants had to wait up because the master and mistress were entertaining or out. In the early years of the 19th century there was no time off except to go to church. However, by the end of the century one day off a month was allowed.

Daily duties
Be downstairs at 6.30 am in the summer and 6.15 am in the winter.
Open shutters first.
Do dining room fire and dust room.
Lay breakfast by 8.15 am.
Dust hall and stairs, morning room and drawing room.
Clear dining room of breakfast dishes.
Make beds.
Answer the door, wait at meals, clear and wash up. Bring in coal as needed.

Weekly jobs
Mon: Wash glass and silver.
Tues: Clean dining room silver.
Wed: Clean hall and polish brass.
Thurs: Polish silver.
Fri: Clean pantry.
Sat: Dust dining room.
Sun: Lay afternoon tea and wash up.

From **Not in front of the Servants.**

Many of the servants worked in service from about the age of ten. It must have been hard to work away from home, with little time to visit the family. There was no legal protection for this large group of the working class, the majority of whom were women.

Everything depended on the goodwill or otherwise of the master or the mistress. Even the best employers regarded servants as belonging to them; some even changed their names if they happened to be the same as one of the family. Mary or Jane were names commonly chosen for them. Rarely did employers take an interest in servants as people. The most important thing was that servants should not get above themselves. But to some extent it was a sheltered and secure life. A servant could be sacked for laziness or being dishonest; but as long as they 'knew their place' and did their work thoroughly, they could be sure of a roof over their heads.

Entertainment for all

The reduction in working hours meant there was more leisure time for most people in the latter years of the 19th century. Wages had also improved for many workers. From 1875 there was also a fall in the cost of living, especially in food prices. All this meant there was a little more money for leisure and entertainment.

Most towns had a theatre where travelling companies performed. The larger cities had music halls where singers and circus acts, conjurors, and even performing animals, entertained the audience. The songs they sang became very popular and were sung at home or in public houses. There were penny concerts and street entertainers, Punch and Judy shows, clowns, peep-shows, street reciters, singers and barrel organs. 'Twopenny hops' were popular with the better-off workers (see Source 7). The circus was also a favourite with all audiences.

For the poorest, who could not afford to buy enough food, let alone a theatre ticket, or even travel on the railway, a penny was enough to get drunk and forget the hard work and troubles of the day.

The middle classes had always had more leisure time, but now more and more people were able to enjoy themselves in new pas-times such as cycling, tennis, hockey or golf. In 1873 the County Cricket Championship began, followed by the first Test Match in 1880. The FA Cup was first played for in 1878 and the Football League began in 1888, with Preston North End the first winners.

As means of transport began to improve, people were able to go further afield and no longer needed to rely on local

SOURCE 7

The numbers present at 'twopenny hops' vary from 30 to 100 of both sexes, their ages being from 15 to 45. At these there is nothing of the leisurely style of dancing, but vigorous, laborious capering.

Henry Mayhew in London's Labour and London Poor, 1851.

SOURCE 8

Love and murder suits us best, sir; but within these few years I think there is a great deal more liking for tragedies among us. They set a man thinking; but then we all consider them too long. Macbeth would be better liked if it was only the witches and the fighting.

We are fond of music. Sailor songs and patriotic songs are liked. A song to take hold of us most has a good chorus. The chorus of 'Britons never shall be slaves' is often rendered 'Britain always shall be slaves'.

A Londoner, speaking to Henry Mayhew. He is describing the ordinary person's taste in entertainment in 1851.

Ramsgate Sands in Kent, a popular seaside resort, painted by William Powell Frith in 1851-3. The railways made it possible for people to visit the seaside on cheap day excursions.

entertainments. They could now go for excursions by train and river steamers or get easily from one part of town to another by omnibus. This greatly contributed to the richness of people's lives.

In the 18th century the upper classes had discovered the pleasures of the seaside. Now the railways enabled working people to take a trip to such resorts as Blackpool, Clacton and Scarborough. Day-trippers went in large numbers and soon piers and promenades were being built for their entertainment. Later, boarding houses were opened for people to stay as the practice of taking an annual holiday began to become more widespread.

There was a steady growth in the number of newly well-off industrialists and shopkeepers. They began to travel abroad. Thomas Cook, who had organized his first outing for a **temperance** meeting, later began to arrange excursions on a more ambitious scale, transporting parties to the continent by rail and steamship. This was the beginning of the travel agency and enabled the new middle class to explore Europe and beyond.

COOK

Thomas Cook (1803–1892) was a sincere Christian and believed in temperance. He had the idea of running a special train to a Temperance Society meeting. It was such a success that he was requested to plan other similar excursions.

Cook was soon to make the organizing of excursions his full-time occupation. He provided information for his customers and made hotel bookings.

Cook issued a monthly magazine called *The Excursionist*, and expanded his business to organizing trips overseas to Europe and America.

Cook lost his sight in later years and his son took over the business, which by 1890 was issuing over three million tickets a year!

Was Britain a better place to live in 1900 than in 1750?

This book describes the many changes which took place in Britain between 1750 and 1900. Were these changes for the better or the worse? This unit may help you come to a conclusion.

During this period numerous inventions had enriched the lives of rich and poor alike. Food was cheaper and more varied; entertainments were more exciting. Education was compulsory for everyone up to the age of twelve and two-thirds of the male adult population had the right to vote. Life expectancy had risen to 46 years for men and 50 years for women.

Yet there was still a long way to go. There was still little state help for ordinary people. There were no old age pensions and most working people were not insured. You simply could not afford to be off work sick or injured at work. Many people still lived on the bread-line and had no disposable income.

Britain in 1750

Britain in 1900

A better place?

Britain in 1750	Britain in 1900
• Small population; most people lived in villages.	• Large population; most people lived in towns.
• Most people worked on the land; some people made cloth in their own houses.	• Most people worked in factories. By 1900, some laws had been passed to protect workers but there was still no National Insurance.
• Little machinery. Energy provided by human muscle, animals, water and wind.	• Factories mechanized; machines driven by steam. Electricity beginning to become important.
• Large wealth gap between the rich and poor.	• Wealth gap narrower but studies showed that one-third of York and London lived in poverty.
• No trade unions.	• Trade unions important; membership increasing.
• No knowledge of germs. No antiseptics or anaesthetics.	• Doctors aware that germs cause diseases. Antiseptics and anaesthetics in use.
• Only a few males could vote.	• Most men could vote. No women could vote.
• Schools available only for the rich.	• Education compulsory and free up to the age of twelve.

SOURCE 2

What is the use of us talking about the British Empire if here, in Britain itself, there is always to be found a mass of people lacking in education, who have little chance of realising in any true sense a good social or domestic life?

Herbert Asquith, a leading Liberal politician, in 1899.

SOURCE 3

Some historians agree that people may have become better-off in terms of wages and goods, but they point to ways in which they were worse-off in terms of **quality of life**.

*C. Culpin, **Making Modern Britain**, 1987.*

SOURCE 4

[The nineteenth century] has seen a whole cycle of changes. The steam engine locomotive by land and sea, steam applied to printing and manufacture, the electric telegraph, photography, cheap newspapers, penny postage, chloroform gas, the electric light, iron ships, revolvers of all sorts, sewing machines, omnibuses and cabs, parcel deliveries, post office savings banks, working men's clubs, people's baths and wash-houses, turkish baths, drinking fountains and a thousand minutiae of daily life, such as matches.

Frances Cobbe, looking back from 1887.

Factory workers on their way to work. This is a still from the television series, **How we used to live, 1851-1901,** broadcast by Yorkshire Television in the 1980s.

SOURCE 6

Historians disagree about the effects of industrialization in the 19th century. Some believe it brought an increase in the standard of living for working people. They argue that wages were higher, food was cheaper and there were greater job opportunities.

Another group of historians say that industrialization brought large towns, squalor, and unhealthy working conditions. They argue that a few people [the factory owners] grew rich at the expense of the workers who were not rewarded enough for their hard work.

From a modern history book, published in 1988.

VICTORIA

Queen Victoria (1819–1901) succeeded to the throne in 1837. At first she relied on her prime minister, Lord Melbourne, for advice but quickly grew in confidence. She had dignity, a strong sense of duty and immense vitality.

In 1840 she married Prince Albert of Saxe-Coberg. She loved him deeply. They had nine children. Their happy domestic life made them popular–especially with the middle classes.

As Prince Consort, Albert worked hard for his adopted country. The Great Exhibition was his greatest triumph. Victoria was heart-broken when he died in 1865 and for many years afterwards would not appear in public.

In her last years, as Empress of India as well as Queen, she was the symbol of the British Empire. Her Diamond Jubilee was a magnificent occasion.

Glossary

apprenticeship a period of time, during which a person learns a trade or craft.

artisan a skilled worker.

British Empire a number of overseas countries which were ruled by Britain. At its height, the British Empire covered one quarter of the world.

census an official count of the population, organized by the government. The first census was held in 1801 and there has been one every ten years since (with the exception of 1941).

cesspit a pit where human waste is deposited.

combine when working people, with the same interests, join together in a friendly society or trade union to support each other.

corves small baskets, used in mines, to carry coal.

factory a large building which houses machinery for making goods. Here large numbers of people work. A factory workforce has to keep regular hours. A model factory has good working conditions, setting an example for others to follow.

French Revolution In 1789, the working people of France, fed up with poor living conditions and high taxes, rebelled against King Louis XVI. In 1793 Louis was guillotined (executed) and France became a republic. The British ruling classes were terrified that the same thing would happen in Britain. They reacted by giving out heavy punishments to people who rioted or complained about their conditions.

gleaning the gathering of ears of corn left behind after a field has been harvested.

hewer a person who digs coal from a coal seam with a pick-axe and shovel.

Industrial Revolution a phrase used by historians to describe the changes which turned Britain from a rural agricultural country to an industrialized country, with steam powered factories and large cities.

Poor Laws laws which dealt with poor people. The Poor Laws were first introduced in the reign of Elizabeth I (1558-1603).

quality of life phrase used to describe how people live in terms of their living conditions, facilities for recreation, the amount of pollution etc.

reform make changes for the better.

3Rs short for reading, writing and arithmetic.

temperance abstaining from alcohol.

tied cottage cottage which goes with a person's job. If workers living in tied cottages lost their job, they also lost their home.

trade depression a period when trade slumps. It is hard to sell goods, profits fall and businesses respond by laying-off or sacking workers. Unemployment, therefore, increases at such times.

workhouse place where people went if they were out of work or unable to support themselves. During the 19th century workhouses had strict rules and a basic diet. They were often feared by working-class people.

'workshop of the world' a phrase used to describe Britain between 1850 and 1875. During this period Britain was the world's leading industrial country.

Index

agriculture 13–15
Althorp's Factory Act (1833) 15, 16
apprenticeship 22
Arkwright, Richard 6
Artisans' Dwellings Act (1875) 20

back to back housing 9, 20
Booth, Charles 23
Bournville 20
British Empire 5, 29
building standards 9, 11

Cadbury, George 20
Chadwick, Edwin 11, 18, 19
Chamberlain, Joseph 20
child labour 6, 7, 12, 13, 16
cholera 11, 18–19
Collieries Act (1842) 16
Cook, Thomas 27
Co-operative Movement 21
cotton cloth 5, 6, 14

Davy, Humphry 13
disease 5, 11, 19, 29
domestic servants 25–6

education 23, 28, 29
Education Acts (1870 and 1902) 23
entertainment 26-7

factories 4, 6–8, 28, 29
Factory Acts 15–17
Fielden, John 6, 7, 15, 17

French Revolution (1789) 14
friendly societies 14

Graham's Act (1844) 17
Grand National Consolidated Trades Union (GNCTU) 14
Great Exhibition (1851) 4–5
Grey's Act (1850) 17

Hill, Octavia 20, 21
housing 5, 20, 29

laissez-faire 15, 16, 18
Lever, William 20
living conditions 5, 9, 10, 13, 18, 22–6, 29–30
Luddites 14

machines 4, 6–7, 13, 14, 16, 28
mechanization 4, 13, 14, 29
middle classes 24–6
mining villages 12
Municipal Corporations Act (1835) 18

Owen, Robert 8

Parliament 15, 17, 18–19. 20–2
Pasteur, Louis 19
Paxton, Joseph 5
Peabody, George 20
population 4, 5, 29
Port Sunlight 20
public health 11

Public Health Acts (1848 and 1875) 18, 19

railways 12, 25, 26, 27
Report on the Sanitary Condition of the Labouring Class 11, 18, 19
Rowntree, Seebohm 23
Rural Rides 7

Sadler, Michael 15
Sale of Food and Drugs Act (1875) 21
Salt, Sir Titus 8, 20
Saltaire 8, 20
Shaftesbury, Earl of 15, 16, 17
Snow, Dr John 19
steam engines 4, 6, 12
Swing Riots (1830) 13, 14

Ten Hours Movement 15
The Times 15
town councils 18, 19
trade depressions 14
trade unions 14–15, 22, 23
travel 27

Victoria, Queen 4, 29, 30
villages 4, 12–13
voting rights 19, 29

wages 9, 13
water supply 9, 18, 29
women at work 16
woollen cloth 4, 13, 14
workhouses 23
working conditions 6–8, 14

Junior Cycle Home Economics

Now You're Cooking!

Recipe and Evaluation Handbook

Julie-Anne Behan & Brenda Fallon Hyland

With a foreword by **Neven Maguire**

Gill Education
Hume Avenue
Park West
Dublin 12
www.gilleducation.ie

Gill Education is an imprint of M.H. Gill & Co.

ISBN: 978-0-7171-88802

Editor: Caitriona Clarke
Design: Sarah McCoy

At the time of going to press, all web addresses were active and
contained information relevant to the topics in this book. Gill Education
does not, however, accept responsibility for the content or views
contained on these websites. Content, views and addresses may change
beyond the publisher or author's control. Students should always be
supervised when reviewing websites.

For permission to reproduce photographs, the authors and publisher
gratefully acknowledge the following:

© Alamy: 2 (xiii), 10, 30, 36, 72, 75, 125, 142, 148, 155B, 168, 178, 181; © iStock: 1, 2,
3, 4, 5, 7, 8, 10, 11, 12, 13, 17, 18, 20, 24, 39, 40, 43, 46, 49, 52, 59, 62, 63, 66, 79, 82,
85, 88, 91, 94, 95, 96, 116, 119, 122, 128, 135, 138, 155T, 158, 162, 165, 171, 184, 195, 200;
© Odlums: 187; © Shutterstock: 2 (xv), 3 (iv), 10, 12, 106, 132; © Steve Brown
Photography: 109; © Stockfood: 23, 33, 55, 131.
All non-credited images have been kindly provided by the authors.

The author and publisher have made every effort to trace all copyright
holders, but if any have been inadvertently overlooked we would be
pleased to make the necessary arrangement at the first opportunity.

The paper used in this book is made from the wood pulp of managed
forests. For every tree felled, at least one tree is planted, thereby renewing
natural resources.

Contents

Foreword by Neven Maguire   v

Introduction   vi

Kitchen Equipment   1

Kitchen Technology   4

Ready to Cook   6

Kitchen Hygiene and Safety   7

Evaluating Cookery Dishes   8

Evaluating Word Bank   9

Cookery Terms and Abbreviations   10

Weighing and Measuring   13

How to Use This Book   14

UNIT 1 BREAKFAST TIME   19

1   Healthy Breakfast Granola   20

2   Pancakes with Simple Blueberry and Banana Sauce   23

3   Silky Smooth Scrambled Eggs and Bacon   26

UNIT 2 SNACKS AND STARTERS   29

4   Smoothies and Milkshakes   30

5   Quesadilla   33

6   Fresh Tomato Pasta   36

7   Garlic Bread and Bruschetta   39

8   Pizza Snack   43

9   Noodle Soup   46

10   Hearty Homemade Vegetable Soup   49

11   Tomato Soup   52

12   Movie Night Treat   55

UNIT 3 HOME BAKING   58

13   Oat Bread   59

14   White and Brown Soda Bread   62

15   Banana Bread   66

16   Coconut Buns   69

17   Scones – Wholemeal/White/Fruit/Savoury/Citrus/Coconut   72

18   Muffins – Lemon and Poppy Seed/Banana/Chocolate Chip/Blueberry   75

19   Queen Cakes   79

20   Simple Cookies   82

21   Special Occasion Chocolate Fudge Cake   85

22   Flapjacks   88

23   Sponge with a Twist   91

24   Pastry – to make Quiche/Apple Tart/Sausage Rolls   94

UNIT 4 DESSERTS   99

25   Chocolate Biscuit Christmas Pudding   100

26   Mini Oreo Cheesecake   103

27   Key Lime Pie   106

28   Trendy Bread and Butter Pudding   109

UNIT 5 MEAT   112

29   Chicken Nuggets and Spicy Potato Wedges   113

30   Stir-Fry for Every Occasion   116

31   Fajitas   119

32   Chicken Tikka Masala   122

33	Deliciously Creamy Paprika Chicken	125
34	Spaghetti Bolognese	128
35	Chilli Two-Ways	131
36	Meatballs in Spicy Tomato Sauce	135
37	Steak Sandwich	138

UNIT 6 FISH — **141**

38	Fish in a Bag	142
39	Layered Fish Bake	145
40	Thai Green Prawn Curry	148
41	Zesty Polenta-Crusted Fish Cakes	151

UNIT 7 FRUIT — **154**

| 42 | Fresh Fruit Salad and Fruit Skewers | 155 |
| 43 | Fruit Crumble | 158 |

UNIT 8 PULSES, VEGETABLES AND SALADS — **161**

44	Coconutty Lentil Curry	162
45	Penne Al'Arrabbiata	165
46	Warm Chicken Salad	168
47	Crispy Smoked Pancetta and Potato Salad	171
48	Summer Salad with Citrus Dressing	174

UNIT 9 MILK, EGGS AND CHEESE — **177**

49	Savoury Omelette	178
50	Garlic Mac and Cheese	181
51	Homemade Cheesy Pizza	184

Costing a Recipe	187
Comparison of Homemade and Commercial Products	188
Practical Skills Exam – Sample Briefs for In-House Exams	189
Working with the Features of Quality	192
Marking Scheme for In-House Exams	193
Food Literacy Skills Brief (CBA 2)	195
Part A – Food Literacy Brief (Sample Layout)	195
Part B – Practical Skills Exam (Sample Layout)	199

Foreword
by Neven Maguire

It is such a pleasure to see this book by Julie-Anne and Brenda. Along with cooking with my mother, Vera, it was in the Home Economics room that my interest in food began, and I am certain that there will be readers of this book who will now begin a lifelong interest in good food, whether that's at home or, perhaps, as a career.

In my day, it was very unusual for a boy to do Home Economics. Thankfully, those days are behind us. The repertoire of recipes in this book will give people a grounding in essential kitchen skills that will see anyone using this book through life if they never cooked another thing. But most will, because also contained in this book is the important skill of being able to look at a recipe and adapt it.

The issues of healthy eating and sustainability are now much more to the fore than when I was training. Every chef is now thinking about food in new ways. I have always been a big fan of eating local food and cooking seasonally, but I also love our new openness to tastes from all over the world. The food served in Irish restaurants and homes has come a long way. And in this day, when fast food is available everywhere, anyone using this book will learn how easy it is to cook something better at home, and something a lot more satisfying!

Home Economics teachers are heroes of mine. You are giving our young people an important foundation, one for which they will be grateful in years to come. There are few better experiences than cooking for and eating with family and friends. This book contains a superb set of building blocks for these skills and these experiences.

Happy cooking!
Neven

Introduction

Now You're Cooking! is the perfect accompaniment to your Junior Cycle Home Economics journey. Through carrying out and evaluating these recipes, you are gaining the key skills required for CBA 2 and the practical skills examination, which is worth 50 per cent of your final result.

The first section gives important information on kitchen equipment, technology, and hygiene and safety. Cooking terms are explained and guidance is given on evaluating dishes.

The recipes included have been carefully chosen to allow for maximum flexibility. They can be adapted to suit a one-hour cookery class and are easily modified for special dietary requirements.

Most importantly, as you fill in your evaluations, you are creating an accurate record of your cookery practicals and evaluations, an invaluable reference point as you complete your Home Economics journey.

The final section of the book gives guidance on costing a recipe and comparing products. Sample Practical Skills Exam briefs and a suggested marking scheme are also given, which will check that all your hard work has prepared you for assessment.

We hope that you enjoy your cookery in Junior Cycle and that these recipes not only inspire you at school, but take you through to college and beyond.

Best of luck,
Brenda and Julie-Anne

Kitchen Equipment

Name and identify at least one use for each of the following pieces of kitchen equipment.

Name: _____ Use: _____ _____ _____	Name: _____ Use: _____ _____ _____	Name: _____ Use: _____ _____ _____	Name: _____ Use: _____ _____ _____
Name: _____ Use: _____ _____ _____	Name: _____ Use: _____ _____ _____	Name: _____ Use: _____ _____ _____	Name: _____ Use: _____ _____ _____
Name: _____ Use: _____ _____ _____	Name: _____ Use: _____ _____ _____	Name: _____ Use: _____ _____ _____	Name: _____ Use: _____ _____ _____
Name: _____ Use: _____ _____ _____	Name: _____ Use: _____ _____ _____	Name: _____ Use: _____ _____ _____	Name: _____ Use: _____ _____ _____
Name: _____ Use: _____ _____ _____	Name: _____ Use: _____ _____ _____	Name: _____ Use: _____ _____ _____	Name: _____ Use: _____ _____ _____

Name: _____

Use: _____

_____

_____

Name: _____

Use: _____

_____

_____

Name: _____

Use: _____

_____

_____

Name: _____

Use: _____

_____

_____

Name: _____

Use: _____

_____

_____

Name: _____

Use: _____

_____

_____

Name: _____

Use: _____

_____

_____

Name: _____

Use: _____

_____

_____

Name: _____

Use: _____

_____

_____

Name: _____

Use: _____

_____

_____

Name: _____

Use: _____

_____

_____

Name: _____

Use: _____

_____

_____

Name: _____

Use: _____

_____

_____

Name: _____

Use: _____

_____

_____

Name: _____

Use: _____

_____

_____

Name: _____

Use: _____

_____

_____

Name: _____

Use: _____

_____

_____

Name: _____

Use: _____

_____

_____

Name: _____

Use: _____

_____

_____

Name: _____

Use: _____

_____

_____

Kitchen Equipment

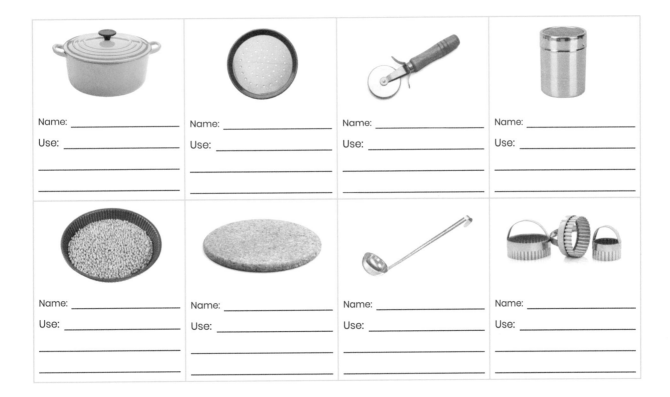

Name: _____	Name: _____	Name: _____	Name: _____
Use: _____	Use: _____	Use: _____	Use: _____

Name: _____	Name: _____	Name: _____	Name: _____
Use: _____	Use: _____	Use: _____	Use: _____

A NOTE ON CHOPPING BOARDS

A chopping board is used to prepare ingredients for cooking. Throughout this book you will be asked to colour-code your chopping boards appropriately (if this is available to you). Here is the colour coding; apply it to every cookery class.

Raw meat Raw fish Salad and fruit Vegetables Bakery and dairy Cooked meat and fish

A NOTE ON ICONS

You will see the following icons used in this book.

 Amount of servings

 Preparation and cooking time

 Reminds you to always wash your hands after preparing or handling raw meat.

 Reminds you to be careful when carrying out this step.

Kitchen Technology

In the Home Economics room you will use many pieces of electrical equipment and appliances. You need to ensure that you use each piece for the right job and that you use it safely. Your teacher will always demonstrate how to use each piece of equipment or appliance.

LARGE APPLIANCES

Name the following large kitchen appliances and identify a use for each.

Name: _____

Use: _____

_____

_____

Name: _____

Use: _____

_____

_____

Name: _____

Use: _____

_____

_____

Name: _____

Use: _____

_____

_____

Name: _____

Use: _____

_____

_____

SMALL EQUIPMENT

Name and identify a use for each of the following pieces of small kitchen equipment. Name one safety issue to be considered when using this appliance.

Name: _____

Use: _____

_____

Safety: _____

_____

Name: _____

Use: _____

_____

Safety: _____

_____

Name: _____

Use: _____

_____

Safety: _____

_____

Name: _____

Use: _____

_____

Safety: _____

_____

Name: _____

Use: _____

_____

Safety: _____

_____

Name: _____

Use: _____

_____

Safety: _____

_____

KITCHEN TECHNOLOGY AND SUSTAINABILITY

Identify two ways in which each of us can contribute to sustainability while using technology in the home, then discuss the issue as a class.

1. _____

_____

2. _____

_____

Ready to Cook

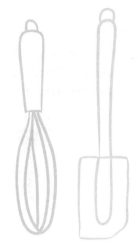

Being ready to cook means that when you enter the kitchen:

1. BAGS are stored away in a safe place.
2. INGREDIENTS are on the table/in the fridge.
3. HANDS are washed and dried with a hand towel.
4. APRONS are on.
5. EQUIPMENT (as listed in your recipe) is collected.
6. UNIT is set up with ingredients and equipment.

Kitchen Hygiene and Safety

Form a class consensus on the rules for kitchen hygiene and safety to be followed.

1. Form groups of four.

2. Each group will take responsibility for one of the following areas: kitchen safety; kitchen hygiene; personal hygiene; food hygiene.

3. In your copy, spend two minutes writing all the rules you can think of under the heading you've been given.

4. Next, take turns to read out your rules to the other members of your group. As a group, add any other rules that you think of.

5. As a class, discuss the rules that each group has come up with. Finalise a set of rules to be agreed upon and followed as a class.

6. Now copy the rules into the boxes below.

KITCHEN HYGIENE	KITCHEN SAFETY
PERSONAL HYGIENE	**FOOD HYGIENE**

Evaluating Cookery Dishes

In the subject of Home Economics, evaluating cookery dishes is an essential component and skill. The word 'evaluate' means to make a judgement on something. In cookery classes, a student will examine the success of the dish prepared, cooked and served in terms of how it was presented, the colour of the dish, the taste and the texture. After considering these key components, a student will then contemplate what changes they would make to the dish to improve it if they were to make it again. In some practical exams, a student may decide that the dish requires no adjustments.

In all Home Economics cookery exams, a written evaluation is a requirement, with a percentage of the marks going for the written evaluation completed during the practical exam. This book has been created with a view to helping and guiding you in developing your cookery and evaluating skills.

When writing your evaluation, the following four categories must be addressed.

COLOUR AND PRESENTATION

How does your dish look? The colours evident in your dish must be described. Make a comment on any garnish used – was this a suitable garnish? Did the dish look attractively presented? Was the dish served hot or cold?

TASTE

How does your dish taste? Each student must sample the dish that was prepared and cooked. When describing the taste of a dish, consider what the predominant flavour of the dish is. It is also important to consider whether or not the dish was well-seasoned. Did the flavours of the dish work well together?

TEXTURE

When evaluating food, the term 'texture' refers to the feel of the food in your mouth. Did it have a hard or soft texture? Lumpy or smooth? Crumbly or dry? Did different components of the dish have different textures?

ANY CHANGES YOU WOULD MAKE

If you were to cook this dish again, are there any changes you would make? Why? For example, if the dish was too sweet, the next time you may choose to reduce the amount of sugar added. If the meat was tough to chew, the next time you may consider a longer and slower method of cooking to result in a more tender piece of meat. If the cake was not well risen, perhaps more raising agent is required.

The word bank on the next page contains a sample of words that can be used to describe the colour, taste and texture of a dish. There is space left in each category to add extra words that you feel are good descriptors.

Evaluating Word Bank

COLOUR	TASTE	TEXTURE
Golden brown	Sweet	Soft
Light brown	Salty	Hard
Pale	Bitter	Lumpy
Brightly coloured	Sour	Smooth
Multi-coloured	Creamy	Spongy
Contrasting colours	Herby	Rough
Colourful	Spicy	Chewy
Dark brown/burnt around the edges	Sugary	Al dente
	Bland	Juicy
	Flavourless	Crunchy
	Buttery	Syrupy
	Fresh	Soggy
	Burnt	Moist
		Sticky
		Tender
		Firm
		Flaky
		Crumbly

Cookery Terms and Abbreviations

Accompaniment

A side dish. Many food dishes are served with a particular food that complements the dish, e.g. curry dishes are often served with rice.

Aeration

A process that involves introducing air into a food product to make it rise, e.g. sieving flour, whisking eggs.

Al dente

A term that describes the firm texture that best suits some foods such as pasta or vegetables.

All-in-one

A quick method for making a cake. All the ingredients are placed in a bowl and mixed together at the same time.

Bake

Process that involves cooking food in an oven with dry heat. Bread and scones are examples of foods that are baked.

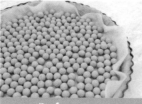

Bake blind

Process that involves baking pastry first without the filling. The filling is added after the period of blind-baking. This helps ensure that the pastry is fully cooked, e.g. quiche.

Boil

To cook food in rapidly bubbling, boiling liquid, e.g. boiling potatoes. Water reaches boiling point at 100° Celsius.

Bouquet garni

A mixture of dried or fresh herbs tied with string or in a muslin bag, added to soups/stews/sauces to give extra flavour. It is removed before eating.

Cream

The mixing of butter/margarine to form a creamy paste. In baking, butter/margarine is often creamed with sugar.

Dice

To cut vegetables or meat into small cube shapes.

Doneness

Term referring to checking when a food item is cooked, which can involve checking the colour and internal temperature of a cut of meat, the moistness or firmness of a baked product, etc.

Dredge

To sprinkle flour on a board or a rolling pin prior to use; can also refer to sprinkling sugar on a baked product.

Fold

A gentle process of incorporating an ingredient through a mixture, in contrast to mixing in an ingredient. Flour, whipped egg white, etc. can be folded in.

Fry

To cook food in a frying pan using a hot oil. Shallow frying = shallow frying pan; deep fat frying = deep fat fryer.

Garnish

A decoration for savoury or sweet dishes, which adds to the overall appearance and taste of the dish, e.g. parsley on soup, mint on dessert.

Glaze

To brush the tops of breads, pastries, scones, etc. with beaten egg or milk prior to them being put in the oven. It results in a glossy, golden colour.

Grate

To cut food into small, thin pieces using a metal grater or a food processor. Grated cheese is a common example.

Grill

To cook food on a grill or a barbecue under/over a dry heat. Radiation is the form of heat transfer involved in grilling.

Julienne

To cut vegetables or meat into long thin strips.

Knead

To stretch and work a dough to help ensure that the gluten is developed. This results in the baked product having a firmer structure.

Knock back

A stage in baking with yeast when the dough is kneaded to 'knock back' or evenly distribute the air bubbles that formed during the first rise throughout the dough. This will result in a more even texture when the dough is baked.

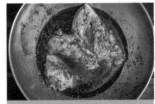

Marinade

To soak meat in food products such as olive oil, vinegar, wine, herbs, etc. before cooking. Such steeping results in a more enhanced flavour and/or a more tender meat.

Pipe

Process whereby royal icing or buttercream is used to decorate baked products by piping it on with a piping bag.

Poach

To cook food gently in liquid at 85ºC (just below boiling point). Fish and fruits are examples of suitable foods for poaching.

Preheat

To heat an oven to the temperature given in the recipe before placing the food item in it. When an oven is switched on, it takes several minutes for it to heat up to the selected temperature. It is important not to place the food in the oven until the set temperature has been reached.

Prove

Process that dough must undergo when yeast is used. The dough is placed in a bowl and covered with cling film or a tea towel and left in a warm place. Fermentation takes place, which results in the production of CO_2. This causes the dough to rise.

Purée

To blend a cooked food such as vegetables to a very smooth, creamy consistency.

Roux sauce

Sauce made from equal quantities of flour and fat (margarine/butter). Varying amounts of liquid (milk) are added depending on how thick or thin the sauce needs to be. This sauce forms the basis for many other sauces, e.g. cheese sauce, parsley sauce, onion sauce.

Rub in

The process of rubbing butter/margarine/lard into flour using the tips of one's fingers. This process is generally carried out until the texture of fine breadcrumbs is achieved.

Sauté

To cook food quickly in small amounts of fat or hot oil.

Season

To add salt, pepper, herbs or spices to a food to improve or enhance the flavour.

Sieve

To pass a product such as flour through a sieve to ensure no lumps are present. This process can also help to aerate the product being made.

Simmer

To cook food gently, just below boiling point.

Steam

To cook food in the steam rising from boiling water.

Stew

To cook food in a little liquid over a gentle heat with the pot or saucepan covered. The liquid is served as part of the dish, e.g. Irish stew.

Stir-fry

To cook food in a little hot fat or oil in a wok. The food is stirred continuously. This is a quick method of cooking.

Stock

A liquid added to soups, sauces, curries, etc. It can be made using a convenience stock cube, to which boiling water is added. Alternatively it can be made from simmering meat bones (e.g. chicken carcass) and/or vegetables in water. The meat bones and vegetables are removed and the flavoured stock can then be used.

Top and tail

To remove the top and bottom parts of vegetables, e.g. carrots, parsnips.

Whisk

Process that involves using a whisk to blend and combine ingredients together. Whisking can also help to incorporate air into the mixture.

Wood of tomato

The part of the tomato that attaches to the stem. It is hard and unpalatable.

Zest

The outer skin of some citrus fruits that can add great flavour to dishes; can be removed by using a vegetable grater or a zester.

ABBREVIATION	EXPLANATION
tsp	teaspoon
tbsp	tablespoon
ml	millilitres
g	grammes
cm	centimetres

Weighing and Measuring

We will measure liquid and solid foods in class.

LIQUIDS

How much water is in each of the jugs?

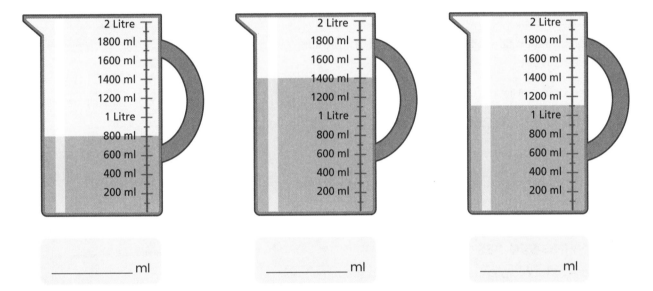

_____ ml   _____ ml   _____ ml

SOLIDS

Weight is measured by using a digital weighing scales. To use the digital scales:

○ Turn it on.

○ Check that the unit of measurement is 'g'.

○ Add the bowl or plate to the scales.

○ 'Tare' the scales – you should now see the number '0'.

○ Start adding the ingredient to the bowl or plate.

○ Watch the display and stop adding the ingredient when you reach the correct weight.

A teaspoon (tsp) should look like this:

If you only need a half a teaspoon, use the knife to scrape half off the spoon.

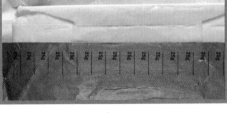

Butter or margarine does not always need to be weighed on the scales. You will see that on the back of the packets there is a convenient scale showing you the quantity in 25-g units.

How to Use This Book

RECIPE PAGE

○ Learning intentions: Link your practical class to the JC specification.

○ Recipe details: Including serving quantity, preparation/cooking times.

○ Suggested modifications/one-hour-class adaptations given where relevant.

○ Ingredients: Full list of ingredients given.

○ Equipment: Full list of equipment given.

○ Method: Complete step-by-step method given.

○ Top tip: Helps you understand the techniques involved, developing your culinary practice.

MODIFYING RECIPES

Modifications for recipes are suggested throughout the book, but others are always possible. When using this book, discuss the ingredients list for each recipe with your teacher in terms of possible modifications. Modifying a recipe is a key skill. It involves adjusting the ingredients list and sometimes the method of cooking. We modify recipes for many reasons, including:

○ special dietary requirements

○ general health (high-fibre diets)

○ eating trends

○ availability of ingredients

○ personal preferences

○ allergies.

ALLERGIES

An allergy is a damaging immune response by the body to a substance, to which it has become hypersensitive. Common food allergies include eggs, tree nuts, peanuts and shellfish. Common allergy symptoms include itchy and watery eyes, itchy and runny nose and sneezing. A severe allergy can result in anaphylaxis, when a person experiences severe breathing difficulties, among other reactions, and this can be life-threatening. It is always important when cooking to consider who you are cooking for and whether they have any food allergies.

EVALUATION PAGE

Q1. Personal reflection: Grade yourself on how well you completed the key skills of the dish. : I did this; I did this in part; I did not do this. This helps you to identify areas in which you have excellent skills as well as skills you might need to improve upon. It will also help you to identify skills where you have shown progression.

Q1. Personal Reflection: Did I ...?

Set up my unit correctly? ☐ ☐ ☐	Stir all ingredients thoroughly? ☐ ☐ ☐
Weigh and measure accurately? ☐ ☐ ☐	Cook the granola until it was golden brown? ☐ ☐ ☐
Preheat the oven to correct temperature? ☐ ☐ ☐	Serve the dish attractively? ☐ ☐ ☐
Choose healthy optional ingredients? ☐ ☐ ☐	Keep a tidy and organised unit throughout? ☐ ☐ ☐
Safely use the hob and oven? ☐ ☐ ☐	Cook and clean within the time available? ☐ ☐ ☐

Q2. Sensory evaluation: Colour, flavour and texture will be evaluated by you for every dish. A critical friend should be consulted by you as often as possible. This is any person who has also tasted your dish. This helps you to understand other people's sensory preferences, and so develop your own understanding of flavour, etc.

Q2. Evaluate your dish using the following headings:

COLOUR _____

_____

FLAVOUR _____

_____

TEXTURE _____

_____

CRITICAL FRIEND _____

_____

Q3. Modifications to your dish: Using the sensory evaluation, suggest improvements you could make to your dish. Explain why these changes are important. If your dish has an excellent sensory evaluation, suggest reasons why this might be/how this occurred.

Q3. Based on your evaluation of the colour, flavour and texture and the comments of your critical friend, identify any changes you would make to your granola.

_____
_____
_____
_____
_____
_____
_____

Q4. Link to cooking principles:
Link theories of cooking principles and techniques to the dish you made in school
or
Hygiene and Safety: Evaluate the specific hygiene and safety rules to help you understand the application of these rules when cooking.

> **Q4. Identify where you applied specific hygiene and safety rules in the preparation and cooking of this dish.**
>
> HYGIENE _____
>
> _____
>
> SAFETY _____
>
> _____

Q5. Optional extension activity: This can be completed where time allows in class or as a homework activity. This question will ask you to investigate how the dish you have cooked links to a balanced diet.

> **Q5. Optional activity: The recommended sugar intake in Ireland per day is 24 g for an adult and 12 g for a child. A recent National Adult Nutritional Survey found that, on average, Irish adults are eating 5 per cent more sugar than is recommended. Write a note on the negative effects of sugar in the diet.**
>
> _____
>
> _____
>
> _____

Q6. Optional extension activity: This can be completed where time allows in class or as a homework activity. The aim of this activity is to deepen your knowledge and understanding of food, nutrition and cooking.

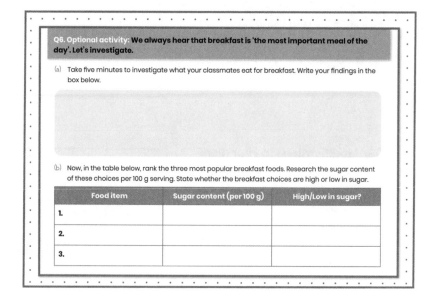

> **Q6. Optional activity: We always hear that breakfast is 'the most important meal of the day'. Let's investigate.**
>
> (a) Take five minutes to investigate what your classmates eat for breakfast. Write your findings in the box below.
>
> (b) Now, in the table below, rank the three most popular breakfast foods. Research the sugar content of these choices per 100 g serving. State whether the breakfast choices are high or low in sugar.
>
> | Food item | Sugar content (per 100 g) | High/Low in sugar? |
> |---|---|---|
> | 1. | | |
> | 2. | | |
> | 3. | | |

COSTING A RECIPE TEMPLATE

This template (p. 187) will help you to learn how to unit-cost a recipe, a skill necessary for your Practical Skills Exam. You should then compare this price to commercially available products and evaluate which product is the best value for money. The aim of this section is to appreciate that homemade foods can be significantly cheaper than commercial varieties.

COMPARISON OF HOMEMADE AND COMMERCIAL PRODUCTS

This template (p. 188) helps you to carry out a complete comparative evaluation between two similar products. An evaluation of sensory attributes and a cost comparison will be completed before evaluating which product was your favourite and why. Again, this skill will be important for your Practical Skills Exam and should be practised regularly.

PRACTICAL SKILLS EXAM – SAMPLE BRIEFS FOR IN-HOUSE EXAMS

These briefs (pp. 189–91) are a sample of what a Food Literacy Skills Brief could look like. Each brief asks you to carry out an investigation, similar to a Food Literacy Skills Brief, and then to carry out the practical component. The written brief and practical component can be assessed as part of in-house cooking exams in First–Third Year. Best practice for teachers would be to assess cooking skills and the written component at end-of-term examinations. Each exam component would merit 50 per cent and the overall result would be an average of these results.

WORKING WITH THE FEATURES OF QUALITY

This document (p. 192) should be used to complete a self and/or peer assessment of the food literacy brief, as issued by the State Examination Commission (SEC). It could also be used for the in-house 'Sample Cookery Exams' to develop the skills necessary for your Food Literacy Brief in Third Year.

MARKING SCHEME FOR IN-HOUSE EXAMS

A sample marking scheme for the above briefs is provided
(pp. 193–4). It can be used by teachers or peers to assess in-house
cookery exams.

FOOD LITERACY SKILLS BRIEF (CBA 2)

Part A: A template for the food literacy brief has been included
(pp. 195–8). The headings in the brief are derived from the features
of quality, as given by the NCCA, but are subject to change over
the next few years as the JC develops. This is used on its own to
complete the Food Literacy Skills Brief.

Part B: A template for the Practical Skills Exam has also been
included (pp. 199–200). The features of quality for this exam have
not been decided at the time of publishing, so these headings are
subject to change.

Both of these templates can be used together to complete in-house
cooking exams in the classroom setting.

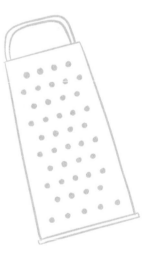

UNIT 1
Breakfast Time

1. **HEALTHY BREAKFAST GRANOLA**

2. **PANCAKES WITH SIMPLE BLUEBERRY AND BANANA SAUCE**

3. **SILKY SMOOTH SCRAMBLED EGGS AND BACON**

1 Healthy Breakfast Granola

Learning Intentions

☆ Use a variety of preparation and cooking techniques to make this dish.

☆ Choose healthy extras to add to the basic recipe.

☆ Apply appropriate hygiene and safety rules when making this dish.

☆ Evaluate the sensory attributes of this dish and its contribution to a healthy diet.

Serves: 4–6   **30–35 mins**

Perfect dish for all class lengths.

Ingredients

200 g porridge oats

25 g coconut oil

25 g honey/golden syrup/maple syrup

OPTIONAL INGREDIENTS: Discuss with your partner and choose 2–3 ingredients from this list to add to the colour/flavour/texture of the granola: 25 g seeds (e.g. sunflower/pumpkin seeds), 25 g dried fruits (e.g. apricots/sultanas/raisins), 50 g nuts (e.g. pecan/brazil/cashew).

Equipment

Chopping board(s) (colour-coded), sharp knife, weighing scales, measuring spoons, mixing bowl, wooden spoon, baking tray, oven gloves, cutlery, two large plates (for cutlery).

Method

1. HANDS, APRON, EQUIPMENT and SET UP UNIT.

2. Preheat the oven to 180°C/gas mark 4.

3. Weigh and measure all ingredients.

4. Prepare your optional ingredients according to the instructions of your teacher. Add these to the mixing bowl.

5. Add the porridge oats to the mixing bowl and mix all ingredients thoroughly.

6. Melt the coconut oil and honey/syrup over a low heat.

7. Pour the melted mixture over the oat mixture and stir thoroughly.

8. Pour onto a baking tray. Place the tray in the oven for 20 mins. Stir once halfway through and cook until golden brown.

9. Remove the granola from the oven using oven gloves, and allow it to cool.

10. Store the granola in an airtight container.

TOP TIP

Granola can be served in many interesting ways for breakfast or for lunch. Try chopped fruit and yogurt topped with granola and drizzled with honey.

Evaluation

Date of Practical: _____

Q1. Personal Reflection: Did I ...?

Set up my unit correctly? ☐ ☐ ☐

Weigh and measure accurately? ☐ ☐ ☐

Preheat the oven to correct temperature? ☐ ☐ ☐

Choose healthy optional ingredients? ☐ ☐ ☐

Safely use the hob and oven? ☐ ☐ ☐

Stir all ingredients thoroughly? ☐ ☐ ☐

Cook the granola until it was golden brown? ☐ ☐ ☐

Serve the dish attractively? ☐ ☐ ☐

Keep a tidy and organised unit throughout? ☐ ☐ ☐

Cook and clean within the time available? ☐ ☐ ☐

Q2. Evaluate your dish using the following headings:

COLOUR _____
_____

FLAVOUR _____
_____

TEXTURE _____
_____

CRITICAL FRIEND _____
_____

Q3. Based on your evaluation of the colour, flavour and texture and the comments of your critical friend, identify any changes you would make to your granola.

_____

_____

_____

_____

_____

_____

_____

_____

Q4. Identify where you applied specific hygiene and safety rules in the preparation and cooking of this dish.

HYGIENE

_____

_____

SAFETY

_____

_____

Q5. Optional activity: The recommended sugar intake in Ireland per day is 24 g for an adult and 12 g for a child. A recent National Adult Nutritional Survey found that, on average, Irish adults are eating 5 per cent more sugar than is recommended. Write a note on the negative effects of sugar in the diet.

_____

_____

_____

Q6. Optional activity: We always hear that breakfast is 'the most important meal of the day'. Let's investigate.

(a) Take five minutes to investigate what your classmates eat for breakfast. Write your findings in the box below.

(b) Now, in the table below, rank the three most popular breakfast foods. Research the sugar content of these choices per 100 g serving. State whether the breakfast choices are high or low in sugar.

Food item	Sugar content (per 100 g)	High/Low in sugar?
1.		
2.		
3.		

2 Pancakes with Simple Blueberry and Banana Sauce

☆ Use a variety of preparation and cooking techniques to make this dish.

☆ Apply appropriate hygiene and safety rules when making this dish.

☆ Evaluate the sensory attributes of this dish and its contribution to a healthy diet.

Serves: 2

45 mins

Makes approx. 4 pancakes

Perfect dish for all class lengths.

Ingredients

FOR THE PANCAKES:

125 g flour

2 eggs

250 ml milk

FOR THE BLUEBERRY AND BANANA SAUCE:

125 g blueberries

2 bananas

1 tbsp water/juice

oil/butter/coconut oil for frying

TOP TIP

If you are worried about your chosen fat making your pancakes greasy, a spray oil can be used for each pancake instead. There is a wide variety of these spray oils available – coconut or olive oil spray both work well.

Equipment

Chopping board(s) (colour-coded), sharp knife, weighing scales, measuring jug, mixing bowl, sieve, whisk, frying pan, ladle, fish slice/ spatula, plate, gravy boat (for sauce), cutlery, two large plates (for cutlery).

Method

1. HANDS, APRON, EQUIPMENT and SET UP UNIT.

2. Weigh and measure all ingredients.

3. Sieve the flour into the mixing bowl.

4. Make a well in the centre and crack in the eggs. Mix with a whisk.

5. Add the milk a little at a time, whisking after each addition to ensure a smooth consistency, until all the milk is added. Set aside.

6. Wash the blueberries, peel and slice the bananas.

7. Add the blueberries, bananas and water/juice to a pot. Bring to the boil, put on the lid and simmer for 3–5 mins until the blueberries are 'bursting' and the bananas have softened but are still holding their shape. Turn off the heat.

8. Bring the pancake batter to the hob.

9. Heat a small amount of the oil/butter/coconut oil in the frying pan.

10. Add a ladleful of batter and carefully lift and tilt the pan to spread the batter so that a thin layer is created.

11. Cook until bubbles appear on top.

12. Flip it over using a fish slice or spatula and cook for another minute. The pancake should be golden in colour.

13. Remove to a clean plate.

14. Repeat steps 9–13 until all the batter is used.

15. Serve pancakes in a stack with the sauce on the side.

Evaluation

Date of Practical: _____

Q1. Personal Reflection: Did I ...?

Set up my unit correctly? ☐ ☐ ☐

Weigh and measure accurately? ☐ ☐ ☐

Mix well after each addition of milk to make a smooth batter? ☐ ☐ ☐

Heat oil/butter until hot? ☐ ☐ ☐

Cook sauce until blueberries have burst and bananas softened but still holding shape? ☐ ☐ ☐

Spread a thin layer of batter around the frying pan? ☐ ☐ ☐

Cook pancakes to a golden colour? ☐ ☐ ☐

Have a well-flavoured end product? ☐ ☐ ☐

Keep a tidy and well-organised unit throughout? ☐ ☐ ☐

Cook and clean within the time available? ☐ ☐ ☐

Q2. Evaluate your dish using the following headings:

COLOUR _____

_____

FLAVOUR _____

_____

TEXTURE _____

_____

CRITICAL FRIEND _____

_____

Q3. Based on your evaluation of the colour, flavour and texture and the comments of your critical friend, identify any changes you would make to your pancakes.

_____

_____

_____

_____

_____

_____

_____

Q4. The pancakes are shallow-fried. List two guidelines to follow when frying.

GUIDELINE 1 _____

_____

GUIDELINE 2 _____

_____

Q6. Optional activity: Build on your skills. Try these at home:

○ Try to flip your pancakes.

○ Find a recipe for 'American style' pancakes and make them.

○ Make this batter suitable for a dairy-free diet/vegan diet using almond milk or coconut milk.

Q5. Optional activity: Fruit has been added to this breakfast dish to make it a balanced meal. Evaluate the nutritive and dietetic contribution of fruit to the diet.

Nutrient	Value in the diet

3 Silky Smooth Scrambled Eggs and Bacon

Serves: 2   **20 mins**

Perfect dish for all class lengths.

Ingredients

4 slices back bacon

4 large eggs (organic are best)

4 tbsp full-fat milk

salt and pepper

25 g pure Irish butter/dairy spread

2 slices wholemeal loaf with a little butter

Equipment

Tongs, measuring jug, fork or whisk, medium-sized non-stick frying pan, wooden spoon, knife, cutlery, two large plates (for cutlery).

TOP TIP

Organic eggs are best used when possible. Garnish this dish with grilled tomato and fresh parsley for an extra healthy option.

Method

1. HANDS, APRON, EQUIPMENT and SET UP UNIT.

2. Preheat the grill to a high temperature.

3. Place the bacon slices on the grill pan and place under the grill once it has reached the desired temperature.

4. Allow the bacon to cook for 5–7 mins before turning, using the tongs, and allow to cook for an additional 3–5 mins depending on the thickness of the bacon.

5. In a measuring jug, gently beat the eggs and milk, being careful not to overwork the mixture, and add the salt and pepper.

6. Heat a medium-sized non-stick frying pan for a minute or two on a medium to high heat.

7. Add the butter and allow it to melt. Do not overheat the butter.

8. Pour the egg mixture into the pan and stir occasionally using a folding action. Do not over-stir.

9. Continue to stir until the egg mixture is cooked through but still soft, then remove from the heat. (It will continue to cook off the heat.)

10. Toast the bread and butter it.

11. Serve the scrambled eggs on top of the buttered toast accompanied by the grilled bacon.

Evaluation

Date of Practical: _____

Q1. Personal Reflection: Did I ...?

Set up my unit correctly? ☐ ☐ ☐

Wash hands after preparing raw meat? ☐ ☐ ☐

Preheat the grill to correct temperature? ☐ ☐ ☐

Turn the bacon during the cooking process? ☐ ☐ ☐

Heat the butter until melted but not overheated? ☐ ☐ ☐

Occasionally stir the eggs while cooking? ☐ ☐ ☐

Use the right cooking times for each ingredient? ☐ ☐ ☐

Have moist, well-cooked bacon? ☐ ☐ ☐

Serve the dish attractively? ☐ ☐ ☐

Have a well-flavoured end product? ☐ ☐ ☐

Keep a tidy and well-organised unit throughout? ☐ ☐ ☐

Cook and clean within the time available? ☐ ☐ ☐

Q2. Evaluate your dish using the following headings:

COLOUR _____

_____

FLAVOUR _____

_____

TEXTURE _____

_____

CRITICAL FRIEND _____

_____

Q3. Based on your evaluation of the colour, flavour and texture and the comments of your critical friend, identify any changes you would make to your scrambled eggs and grilled bacon.

_____

_____

_____

_____

Q4. The eggs in this dish have been scrambled. Name two other ways of cooking eggs.

1. _____

2. _____

Q5. Optional activity: Eggs are a nutritious food. Evaluate the nutritional contribution of eggs to our diet. Include four points of information.

Nutritional and dietetic value of eggs
1.
2.
3.
4.

Q6. Optional activity: In groups of three, nominate a different person for each of the following roles:

○ Note-keeper: Record the group's opinions.

○ Reporter: Report the findings of the group back to the rest of the class.

○ Time-keeper: Keep time.

Now discuss these questions in your group:

1. Explain your understanding of the term 'locally produced'.

2. How does buying locally produced goods benefit the sustainability of our communities and environment?

3. In your opinion, are there any ethical issues to consider when buying eggs?

UNIT 2
Snacks and Starters

4. **SMOOTHIES AND MILKSHAKES**

5. **QUESADILLA**

6. **FRESH TOMATO PASTA**

7. **GARLIC BREAD AND BRUSCHETTA**

8. **PIZZA SNACK**

9. **NOODLE SOUP**

10. **HEARTY HOMEMADE VEGETABLE SOUP**

11. **TOMATO SOUP**

12. **MOVIE NIGHT TREAT**

UNIT 2

4 Smoothies and Milkshakes

Serves: 2   **10 mins**

Perfect dish for all class lengths.

This would also be an ideal recipe to prepare when cooking the quesadillas (see Recipe 5).

(see Recipe 5)

Learning Intentions

☆ Demonstrate the correct culinary techniques required to prepare, cook and serve these drinks.

☆ Choose ingredients to make these drinks.

☆ Apply appropriate hygiene and safety rules when making these drinks.

☆ Evaluate the sensory attributes of these drinks.

☆ Compare fresh and frozen fruit.

Smoothies

Ingredients

150 g frozen or fresh fruit. Banana, berries, mango, kiwis, peaches, plums, melon and nectarines all work well. (If the fruits being used are a little sour, 1 to 2 teaspoons of honey or maple syrup can be added to sweeten the smoothie.)

300 ml juice

125 ml yogurt

fresh mint (optional, to garnish)

Equipment

Chopping board(s) (colour-coded), sharp knife, weighing scales/jug, peeler, food blender/smoothie maker/hand blender, tall serving glass, paper/metal straw, cutlery, two large plates (for cutlery).

Method

1. HANDS, APRON, EQUIPMENT and SET UP UNIT.

2. Weigh the fruit.

3. Measure the yogurt and fruit juice.

4. Wash or peel and roughly chop the fruit. Do not forget to remove the stones from the fruit.

5. Put the fruit, juice and yogurt in the food blender/smoothie maker and blend until it is smooth. If you do not have a food blender/smoothie maker, put the ingredients in a large bowl and blend using a hand blender.

6. Serve in a tall chilled glass with a straw. Garnish with a sprig of fresh mint.

TOP TIP

Smoothies are very quick to make. Remember that other ingredients can also be added such as oats, spinach, avocado and flaxseeds to further increase the nutritional benefits of the drink.

Milkshakes

Ingredients

250 ml milk

Choose one of the following: 2 bananas/200 g strawberries/200 g raspberries

1 tsp honey (organic if possible)

2 generous scoops vanilla ice cream (or another preferred flavour)

Equipment

Chopping board(s) (colour-coded), sharp knife, weighing scales/jug, peeler, food blender/smoothie maker/hand blender, tall serving glass, paper/metal straw, cutlery, two large plates (for cutlery).

Method

1. HANDS, APRON, EQUIPMENT and SET UP UNIT.

2. Measure the milk.

3. Weigh, wash, peel and roughly chop the fruit.

4. Put the milk, fruit, honey and ice cream into a food blender/smoothie maker and blend. Alternatively a large bowl and a hand blender can be used. Blend until a frothy consistency is evident.

5. Serve in a tall chilled glass with a straw. Choose a garnish that complements your milkshake, such as coloured sprinkles, a dusting of coffee essence or an orange slice.

TOP TIP

If you prefer a thick milkshake, use less milk. For a thinner milkshake, add more milk. Milkshakes can be topped with whipped cream, but remember that cream is high in saturated fats.

Evaluation

Date of Practical: _____

Q1. Personal Reflection: Did I ...?

Set up my unit correctly? ☐ ☐ ☐

Weigh and measure my ingredients accurately? ☐ ☐ ☐

Chop the fruit roughly? ☐ ☐ ☐

Measure the milk/juice correctly? ☐ ☐ ☐

Place all the ingredients in the blender/smoothie maker and blend until smooth? ☐ ☐ ☐

Apply the correct safety techniques when using the food blender/smoothie maker/hand blender? ☐ ☐ ☐

Serve the drink attractively? ☐ ☐ ☐

Have a well-flavoured end product? ☐ ☐ ☐

Keep a tidy and well-organised unit throughout? ☐ ☐ ☐

Prepare, serve and clean within the time available? ☐ ☐ ☐

Q2. Evaluate your drinks using the following headings:

COLOUR _____

_____

FLAVOUR _____

_____

TEXTURE _____

_____

CRITICAL FRIEND _____

_____

Q3. Based on your evaluation of the colour, flavour and texture and the comments of your critical friend, identify any changes you would make to your drinks.

_____

_____

_____

_____

_____

_____

_____

Q4. Name a piece of electrical equipment that you used to make your smoothie/ milkshake.

_____

_____

Q5. Optional activity: Frozen fruits can be used to make smoothies. In the box below, carry out a sensory comparison between fresh fruit and frozen fruit.

Compare	Fresh fruit	Frozen fruit
Colour		
Taste		
Texture		
Cost per 100 g		
Any other notes		

Q6. Optional activity: In groups of two–three, and referring back to the Smoothie Top Tip, develop an alternative smoothie to the one developed in class that would be suitable for an active sportsperson.

○ List the ingredients your group will use to make this smoothie.

○ Briefly research the health benefits of the ingredients you have chosen to include for the sportsperson.

○ Present your findings to your class.

5 Quesadilla

Serves: 2   **30 mins**

A one-hour class may not be sufficient to make one of the suggested accompaniments, but if the class is longer, choose and prepare an accompaniment.

Ingredients

50 g grated cheese

Choose ingredients to make this a balanced snack (three food groups):

½ pepper

1 tomato

1 spring onion

6 olives

1 tbsp tinned pineapple

1 slice cold cooked meat/
1 small tin of tuna

2 flour or corn tortillas

ACCOMPANIMENT:
Tomato salsa, side salad, guacamole and/or potato wedges

Equipment

Chopping board(s) (colour-coded), sharp knife, grater, tin opener, frying pan, fish slice, cutlery, two large plates (for cutlery).

Method

1. HANDS, APRON, EQUIPMENT and SET UP UNIT.
2. Grate the cheese.
3. Wash all salad ingredients.
4. Deseed, slice and dice the pepper.
5. Halve the tomato, remove and discard the wood, slice and dice it.
6. Top and tail the spring onion and chop into fine circles.
7. Slice the meat into small pieces/strain the tin of tuna.
8. Heat a dry frying pan to a medium heat.
9. Add the tortilla to the pan and add ingredients to one half of the tortilla only.
10. Sprinkle half the cheese on the tortilla and warm this gently on the pan until the cheese starts to melt.
11. Build the quesadilla by adding the meat/tuna and salad. Now add the remaining cheese and fold over the tortilla.
12. Flip the quesadilla carefully using the fish slice and cook the other side. Both sides should be golden in colour.
13. Remove from the pan.
14. Cut into wedges and serve on a plate with your chosen accompaniment.

TOP TIP
This is an ideal way to use up leftover meat, fish or salad, and so avoid food waste.

TOP TIP
Add ingredients on one half of the tortilla only. This makes it easier to fold the quesadilla over before flipping it.

Evaluation

Date of Practical: _____

Q1. Personal Reflection: Did I ...?

Set up my unit correctly? ☐ ☐ ☐

Choose ingredients to make a balanced snack? ☐ ☐ ☐

Use the grater safely? ☐ ☐ ☐

Dice and chop the ingredients finely? ☐ ☐ ☐

Use a medium heat throughout? ☐ ☐ ☐

Gently melt the cheese inside the quesadilla? ☐ ☐ ☐

Heat all the remaining ingredients thoroughly? ☐ ☐ ☐

Achieve a golden colour on the tortilla? ☐ ☐ ☐

Serve the dish attractively? ☐ ☐ ☐

Keep a tidy and well-organised unit throughout? ☐ ☐ ☐

Prepare, serve and clean within the time available? ☐ ☐ ☐

Q2. Evaluate your dish using the following headings:

COLOUR _____

_____

FLAVOUR _____

_____

TEXTURE _____

_____

CRITICAL FRIEND _____

_____

Q3. Based on your evaluation of the colour, flavour and texture and the comments of your critical friend, identify any changes you would make to your quesadilla.

_____

_____

_____

_____

_____

_____

_____

_____

Q4. Identify where you applied specific hygiene and safety rules in the preparation and serving of this dish.

HYGIENE _____

_____

SAFETY _____

_____

Q5. Optional activity: You were asked to make this a balanced snack. A balanced snack has at least three food groups. Name the ingredients you used and identify their food groups.

Ingredient	Food group

Q6. Optional activity: A quesadilla is a traditional Mexican dish that is a popular modern take on a toasted sandwich. Eating trends change regularly in society. In small groups, research three reasons for changes in eating trends.

1. _____

   _____

2. _____

   _____

3. _____

   _____

6 Fresh Tomato Pasta

Serves: 4   **35 mins**

If the class exceeds one hour, grate the cheese and toast some pine nuts to add to the complexity of this dish.

Ingredients

400 g pasta

2 tbsp olive oil

salt and pepper

3 tomatoes/12–15 baby tomatoes (if using baby tomatoes, try using different coloured ones)

large handful fresh basil leaves

2 cloves garlic

2 tbsp pesto

parmesan/cheddar cheese

OPTIONAL:
pepperoni slices

Equipment

Chopping board(s) (colour-coded), sharp knife, medium-sized saucepan, wooden spoon, garlic crusher, grater, large bowl, colander, cutlery, two large plates (for cutlery).

Method

1. HANDS, APRON, EQUIPMENT and SET UP UNIT.

2. Bring a saucepan of water to the boil.

3. Add the pasta to the saucepan with a pinch of salt and a tablespoon of oil.

4. Stir the pasta and boil for 12 mins.

5. While the pasta is cooking, prepare the vegetables. Wash the tomatoes, remove and discard the wood (large tomatoes only) and dice finely; chop the basil finely; and peel and crush the garlic. Mix these ingredients together in a large bowl with the salt, pepper and a tablespoon of oil.

6. Test the pasta for doneness. When the pasta starts to come to the surface of the water and has swollen, it is ready for checking. Remove one piece from the water and cut it in half. If it is done, the centre of the pasta will be uniform in colour.

7. Strain the pasta using the colander. ⚠

8. Add the pasta and pesto to the tomato mixture and gently stir together.

9. Grate the cheese over the pasta and serve.

> **TOP TIP**
>
> Cooking pasta to perfection is a key skill to learn. Be comfortable with how to test pasta for doneness – it should be perfectly al dente.

Evaluation

Date of Practical: _____

Q1. Personal Reflection: Did I ...?

Set up my unit correctly? ☐ ☐ ☐

Use my knife safely? ☐ ☐ ☐

Use the grater safely? ☐ ☐ ☐

Add pasta to boiling water? ☐ ☐ ☐

Cook pasta until al dente? ☐ ☐ ☐

Strain the pasta without risk of scalding myself? ☐ ☐ ☐

Chop tomatoes and basil finely? ☐ ☐ ☐

Have a well-flavoured end product? ☐ ☐ ☐

Serve the dish attractively? ☐ ☐ ☐

Keep a tidy and well-organised unit throughout? ☐ ☐ ☐

Prepare, serve and clean within the time available? ☐ ☐ ☐

Q2. Evaluate your dish using the following headings:

COLOUR _____

_____

FLAVOUR _____

_____

TEXTURE _____

_____

CRITICAL FRIEND _____

_____

Q3. Based on your evaluation of the colour, flavour and texture and the comments of your critical friend, identify any changes you would make to your fresh tomato pasta.

_____
_____
_____
_____
_____
_____
_____

Q4. Identify where you applied specific hygiene and safety rules in the preparation and serving of this dish.

HYGIENE _____
_____

SAFETY _____
_____

Q5. Optional activity: Pasta is most commonly made from the wheat grain. Draw and label a diagram of a wheat grain below.

Q6. Optional activity: Fresh pasta is considered superior in quality to dried pasta. It is increasingly available in supermarkets today.

(a) Research the advantages and disadvantages of using fresh pasta in cooking.

Advantages	Disadvantages

(b) Investigate and compare the cost of 100 g of fresh and 100 g of dried pasta.

Fresh pasta price per 100 g: _____

Dried pasta price per 100 g: _____

7 Garlic Bread and Bruschetta

Serves: 2

15 mins

Perfect dish for all class lengths.

Garlic bread and bruschetta could both be achieved in a one-hour class.

Learning Intentions

☆ Demonstrate the correct culinary techniques required to prepare and cook these dishes.

☆ Apply appropriate hygiene and safety rules when making these dishes.

☆ Evaluate the sensory attributes of these dishes.

☆ Complete a sensory comparison between a homemade and shop-bought product.

Garlic Bread

TOP TIP

All different types of bread can be used to make garlic bread, and the oven can be used instead of the grill.

Ingredients

1 small ciabatta

2 cloves garlic

2 tbsp fresh parsley

50 g butter/dairy spread

OPTIONAL:
2 tbsp grated parmesan/ Cheddar cheese

Equipment

Chopping board(s) (colour-coded), chopping knife, garlic crusher, fork, bowl, knife, baking tray, cutlery, two large plates (for cutlery).

Method

1. HANDS, APRON, EQUIPMENT and SET UP UNIT.
2. Preheat the grill to a high temperature.
3. Cut the ciabatta in two lengthways.
4. Peel and crush the garlic and chop the parsley.
5. Mix the butter, garlic and most of the parsley together in a bowl, ensuring there is an even distribution of garlic and parsley in the butter.
6. Lightly toast the ciabatta for 2 mins under the grill, then reduce the heat of the grill to medium.
7. Spread the garlic and parsley butter over each slice of ciabatta.
8. Sprinkle over the cheese (if using).
9. Place on a baking tray and place back under the grill until the butter has melted and the toast is golden. Watch closely – this can burn very quickly.
10. Serve hot and garnish with the remaining parsley.

Bruschetta

Ingredients

2 large tomatoes

1 small red onion

1 clove garlic

1 small ciabatta

4 tbsp olive oil

1 tbsp balsamic vinegar

salt and black pepper

4 fresh basil leaves
(to garnish)

Equipment

Chopping board(s) (colour-coded), sharp knife, bowl, pastry brush, tablespoon, cutlery, two large plates (for cutlery).

Method

1. HANDS, APRON, EQUIPMENT and SET UP UNIT.

2. Preheat the grill to a high temperature.

3. Cut the tomatoes in two, remove and discard the wood, dice and place in the bowl.

4. Peel and finely chop the red onion and mix with the tomatoes.

5. Peel the garlic and cut in two lengthways.

6. Cut the ciabatta in two lengthways. Brush the ciabatta lightly with olive oil on both sides.

7. Grill the ciabatta on both sides, under a medium heat, until lightly charred.

8. Rub one side of each ciabatta with the cut garlic.

9. Top each slice with the tomatoes and red onion mix. Drizzle a little olive oil and balsamic vinegar over each. Season with salt and pepper.

10. Garnish with basil leaves and serve immediately.

TOP TIP

Whether you have a large garden or a small balcony, fresh herbs such as parsley and basil are easily grown. They add wonderful flavour to home-cooked meals.

Evaluation

Date of Practical: _____

Q1. Personal Reflection: Did I ...?

Set up my unit correctly? ☐ ☐ ☐

Peel and chop/dice/crush the ingredients? ☐ ☐ ☐

Preheat the grill to correct temperature? ☐ ☐ ☐

(Garlic bread) Evenly distribute the chopped garlic and chopped parsley in the butter? ☐ ☐ ☐

(Garlic bread) Lightly toast the ciabatta before spreading the garlic butter? ☐ ☐ ☐

(Garlic bread) Grill the garlic butter ciabatta under a medium-heat grill? ☐ ☐ ☐

(Bruschetta) Peel and dice/finely chop the tomatoes/onion? ☐ ☐ ☐

(Bruschetta) Grill the ciabatta on both sides until lightly charred, and top with diced tomato and red onion? ☐ ☐ ☐

(Bruschetta) Drizzle olive oil and balsamic vinegar over each slice? ☐ ☐ ☐

Have a well-flavoured end product? ☐ ☐ ☐

Keep a tidy and well-organised unit throughout? ☐ ☐ ☐

Prepare, serve and clean within the time available? ☐ ☐ ☐

Q2. Evaluate your dishes using the following headings:

COLOUR _____

_____

FLAVOUR _____

_____

TEXTURE _____

_____

CRITICAL FRIEND _____

_____

Q3. Based on your evaluation of the colour, flavour and texture and the comments of your critical friend, identify any changes you would make to your garlic bread and bruschetta.

_____

_____

_____

_____

_____

_____

_____

Q4. Identify where you applied specific hygiene and safety rules in the preparation and serving of these dishes.

HYGIENE _____

_____

SAFETY _____

_____

Q5. Optional activity: Plan a three-course main meal with garlic bread or bruschetta as the starter. Ensure this menu is balanced (three food groups).

MENU

Starter

Main Course and Drink

Dessert

Balanced Food Check

Fruit/Veg
☐

Breads/Cereals
☐

Dairy
☐

Meat/Alternatives
☐

Q6. Optional activity: As a class, complete a sensory comparison between shop-bought garlic bread and homemade garlic bread. While making your garlic bread, cook one shop-bought garlic bread. Then compare the garlic breads using the following headings:

Compare	Homemade garlic bread	Shop-bought garlic bread
Colour		
Taste		
Texture		
Cost per 100 g (use the costing template on p. 187)		
Any other notes		

8 Pizza Snack

Serves: 2–4 **45 mins**

In a one-hour class, choose toppings that need little preparation time.

Ingredients

1 onion

1 clove garlic

1 tbsp oil

1 tin tomatoes
2 tbsp tomato purée } or 400 ml passata

½ tsp basil

½ tsp oregano

Choose your toppings:
ham, chicken, sweetcorn, chopped pineapple, peppers, olives, red onion, chilli, mushrooms, pepperoni, etc.

1 medium French bread/2 wraps/2 pitta breads

100 g grated cheese

fresh basil (to garnish)

Equipment

Chopping board(s) (colour-coded), sharp knife, garlic crusher, tin opener, saucepan with lid, wooden spoon, plate for toppings, baking tray, oven gloves, cutlery, two large plates (for cutlery).

Method

1. HANDS, APRON, EQUIPMENT and SET UP UNIT.

2. Preheat the oven to 180°C/gas mark 4.

3. Peel and dice the onion and peel and crush the garlic.

4. Heat the oil in a saucepan and sauté the onion and garlic for 5 mins.

5. Add tomatoes, tomato purée/passata, basil and oregano. Raise the heat and bring to a boil. Reduce the heat and simmer for 10 mins.

6. While the sauce is cooking, prepare the toppings you will use.

7. Cut the French bread in two lengthways. (Alternatively, use wraps or pitta bread as your pizza base.)

8. Spread a generous amount of the cooked tomato sauce on top of the bread base.

9. Arrange the toppings attractively and then sprinkle the cheese on top.

10. Put the pizza onto a baking tray and bake for 10 mins until the cheese is golden. Remove using oven gloves.

11. Serve garnished with some fresh basil.

TOP TIP

Once ready, the sauce can be blended with a hand blender to make it smooth. If you have sauce left over, keep it and mix it with pasta for dinner.

Evaluation

Date of Practical: _____

Q1. Personal Reflection: Did I ...?

Set up my unit correctly? ☐ ☐ ☐

Dice the onion evenly using the correct technique? ☐ ☐ ☐

Heat oil until hot? ☐ ☐ ☐

Sauté using correct temperature until onion was soft? ☐ ☐ ☐

Use correct temperature control throughout? ☐ ☐ ☐

Prepare the toppings correctly? ☐ ☐ ☐

Assemble pizza in the correct sequence? ☐ ☐ ☐

Arrange toppings attractively and bake until the cheese was golden? ☐ ☐ ☐

Keep a tidy and well-organised unit throughout? ☐ ☐ ☐

Prepare, serve and clean within the time available? ☐ ☐ ☐

Q2. Evaluate your dish using the following headings:

COLOUR _____

_____

FLAVOUR _____

_____

TEXTURE _____

_____

CRITICAL FRIEND _____

_____

Q3. Based on your evaluation of the colour, flavour and texture and the comments of your critical friend, identify any changes you would make to your pizza snack.

_____

_____

_____

_____

Q4. Identify where you applied specific hygiene and safety rules in the preparation and serving of this dish.

HYGIENE _____

_____

_____

SAFETY _____

_____

_____

Q5. Optional activity: Many different breads can be used to make these pizza snacks. List a different nutritive advantage of each of the following breads.

Bread	Nutritive advantage
White bread roll	
Pitta bread	
Seeded wrap	
Wholemeal roll	

Q6. Optional activity: With your partner, design a 'pizza face' that you could make for a children's pizza party using a range of healthy toppings.

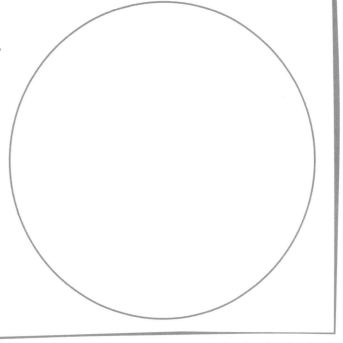

9 Noodle Soup

Serves: 6

40 mins

Perfect dish for all class lengths.

Ingredients

1 onion

2 carrots

small packet green beans

2 stalks celery

1 litre chicken stock (made using 1 chicken stock cube)

1 tbsp oil

1 tin tomatoes

2 noodle nests/straight to wok noodles of your choice

salt and pepper

fresh coriander

OPTIONAL:
1 clove garlic/1 fresh chilli/ 1 tsp Chinese five spice

Equipment

Chopping board(s) (colour-coded), sharp knife, peeler, grater, measuring jug, whisk/fork, tin opener, large saucepan with lid, wooden spoon, soup tureen and serving spoon/ladle, cutlery, two large plates (for cutlery).

Method

1. HANDS, APRON, EQUIPMENT and SET UP UNIT.

2. Peel and finely dice the onion.

3. Peel and dice/grate the carrots.

4. Wash the green beans, remove and discard stalks and chop into small pieces.

5. Wash, top, tail and dice the celery.

6. Make the stock by adding 1 litre of boiling water to a chicken stock cube and stirring until the stock cube has dissolved.

7. Peel and crush the garlic (if using). Halve, de-seed and finely slice the chilli (if using). (Always make sure to wash your hands after handling chilli and be sure not to rub your eyes or put your hands near your face after handling and preparing it, as the oil-like capsaicin in the chilli will burn.)

8. Heat the oil in a large saucepan. Check that it is hot by adding a piece of onion and waiting for it to sizzle.

9. Add all the vegetables (and garlic, chilli or Chinese five spice). Turn the heat down low, put the lid on the saucepan and sauté the vegetables for 5–7 mins.

10. Raise the heat. Add the tomatoes and stock. Bring the soup to the boil. Boil for 2 mins.

11. Add the noodles and cook for 3 mins. Be sure not to overcook the noodles. Taste and add salt/pepper if needed.

12. Serve in a soup tureen and garnish with fresh coriander.

TOP TIP

This soup is not blended. Ensure your dicing is fine and even to make it visually attractive. Keep working on this skill at home as well as in school!

Evaluation

Date of Practical: _____

Q1. Personal Reflection: Did I ...?

Set up my unit correctly? ☐ ☐ ☐

Dice my vegetables evenly? ☐ ☐ ☐

Make the correct amount of stock? ☐ ☐ ☐

Heat the oil until hot? ☐ ☐ ☐

Sauté the vegetables until soft? ☐ ☐ ☐

Use correct temperature control throughout? ☐ ☐ ☐

Avoid overcooking the noodles? ☐ ☐ ☐

Have a well-flavoured end product? ☐ ☐ ☐

Keep a tidy and well-organised unit throughout? ☐ ☐ ☐

Prepare, serve and clean within the time available? ☐ ☐ ☐

Q2. Evaluate your dish using the following headings:

COLOUR _____

_____

FLAVOUR _____

_____

TEXTURE _____

_____

CRITICAL FRIEND _____

_____

Q3. Based on your evaluation of the colour, flavour and texture and the comments of your critical friend, identify any changes you would make to your noodle soup.

_____

_____

_____

_____

_____

_____

_____

_____

Q5. Optional activity: Many types of noodles are available in our supermarkets; however, many of them are unsuitable for a gluten-free diet. List two modifications that could be made to make this soup suitable for a gluten-free diet.

1. _____

_____

2. _____

_____

Q4. Identify where you applied specific hygiene and safety rules in the preparation and serving of this dish.

HYGIENE _____

_____

_____

SAFETY _____

_____

_____

Q6. Optional activity: From your study of Home Economics, recap on the term 'sauté'.

(a) Define the term 'sauté'.

(b) List guidelines for how to complete this cooking process effectively.

(c) What is the advantage of cooking foods in this way?

Definition
Guidelines
Advantage

10 Hearty Homemade Vegetable Soup

Learning Intentions

☆ Choose ingredients to make a healthy soup.

☆ Demonstrate the correct culinary techniques required to prepare and cook this dish.

☆ Apply appropriate hygiene and safety rules when making this dish.

☆ Discuss the contribution of homemade soup in helping to prevent food waste.

☆ Evaluate the sensory attributes of this dish and examine its contribution to a healthy diet.

Serves: 4   **55 mins**

In a one-hour class, reduce the quantities used.

Ingredients

1 medium potato (helps to thicken the soup)

1 onion/1 leek (for flavour)

550 g chopped vegetables – choose a selection from the following suggestions:

sweet potato, carrots, parsnips, peppers, mushrooms, onions, leeks, potato, tomatoes, celery, butternut squash, sweetcorn

1 clove garlic

850 ml stock (chicken/vegetable)

1 tbsp cooking oil/olive oil

1 bouquet garni/dried mixed herbs

salt and pepper

parsley and cream (optional, to garnish)

Equipment

Chopping board(s) (colour-coded), sharp knife, weighing scales, peeler, garlic crusher, measuring jug, whisk/fork, large saucepan, wooden spoon, pot stand, hand blender, serving bowl and spoon, cutlery, two large plates (for cutlery).

Method

1. HANDS, APRON, EQUIPMENT and SET UP UNIT.

2. Weigh and measure ingredients. (If you do not have access to a weighing scales, just ensure when adding the stock that it covers the vegetables by at least 2"/6 cm.)

3. Wash, peel and chop the vegetables.

4. Peel and crush the garlic.

5. Make the stock by adding 850 ml of boiling water to a chicken or vegetable stock cube and stirring until the stock cube has dissolved. Alternatively, use homemade vegetable or chicken stock.

6. Heat the oil, add the vegetables and garlic and sauté for about 5 mins, stirring continuously until vegetables begin to soften.

7. Add the stock and bouquet garni.

8. Bring to the boil, cover and reduce heat. Simmer gently for 25–30 mins until vegetables are cooked through.

9. Remove from the heat, place the saucepan on a pot stand and liquidise with a hand blender.

10. Season with salt and pepper to taste.

11. Serve hot and garnish with some fresh parsley or a dollop of cream.

TOP TIP

Soup is very good value to make as inexpensive vegetables can be used to make a healthy and nutritious dish. Leftover vegetables can also be used, which is a great example of a sustainable food practice that can be implemented in our homes.

Evaluation

Date of Practical: _____

Q1. Personal Reflection: Did I ...?

Set up my unit correctly? ☐ ☐ ☐

Heat oil until hot? ☐ ☐ ☐

Sauté the vegetables until they began to soften? ☐ ☐ ☐

Add ingredients in the correct order? ☐ ☐ ☐

Simmer the soup for the correct length of time? ☐ ☐ ☐

Apply the correct safety procedures when liquidising the soup? ☐ ☐ ☐

Season the soup correctly? ☐ ☐ ☐

Have a well-flavoured end product? ☐ ☐ ☐

Keep a tidy and well-organised unit throughout? ☐ ☐ ☐

Prepare, serve and clean within the time available? ☐ ☐ ☐

Q2. Evaluate your dish using the following headings:

COLOUR _____

_____

FLAVOUR _____

_____

TEXTURE _____

_____

CRITICAL FRIEND _____

_____

Q3. Based on your evaluation of the colour, flavour and texture and the comments of your critical friend, identify any changes you would make to your vegetable soup.

_____

_____

_____

_____

Q4. Boiling is one of the cooking method used in this recipe. Identify two guidelines to follow when using this method of cooking.

GUIDELINE 1 _____

_____

GUIDELINE 2 _____

_____

Q5. Optional activity: Homemade vegetable soup is naturally high in fibre. Outline three functions of fibre in the diet.

1. _____

_____

2. _____

_____

3. _____

_____

Q6. Optional activity: By using homemade stock, further nutritional value is added to our soups. Chicken or vegetable stock can be made very simply. In pairs:

(a) Research how to make a homemade vegetable or chicken stock.

(b) Identify the benefits of using homemade stock.

11 Tomato Soup

☆ Use a variety of preparation and cooking techniques to make this dish.

☆ Apply appropriate hygiene and safety rules when making this dish.

☆ Demonstrate creative skills by choosing and using a suitable garnish for serving.

☆ Evaluate the sensory attributes of this dish and examine its contribution to a healthy diet.

☆ Use food labels to evaluate nutritional content of commercially available foods.

Serves: 4

45 mins

Perfect dish for all class lengths.

Ingredients

1 potato

1 onion

2 cloves garlic

2 sticks celery

500 ml chicken/vegetable stock

1 tbsp olive oil

1 tbsp tomato purée

1 tin tomatoes

1 tsp sugar (optional)

salt and pepper

cream/croutons/fresh basil/1 tbsp pesto (to garnish)

Equipment

Chopping board(s) (colour-coded), sharp knife, peeler, garlic crusher, measuring jug, whisk/fork, tin opener, large saucepan, wooden spoon, pot stand, hand blender, soup tureen and serving spoon/ladle, cutlery, two large plates (for cutlery).

TOP TIP

Sugar is an optional ingredient in this tomato-based dish. Its function is to balance the acidity of the tomato flavours. A very small amount is sufficient but you can choose to leave it out if you are following a low-calorie/low-sugar diet.

Method

1. HANDS, APRON, EQUIPMENT and SET UP UNIT.

2. Peel and dice the potato and onion.

3. Peel and crush the garlic.

4. Wash, top, tail and dice the celery.

5. Make the stock by adding 500 ml of boiling water to the stock cube and stirring until the stock cube has dissolved.

6. Heat the oil in a large saucepan. Check that it is hot by adding a piece of onion and waiting for it to sizzle.

7. Add all vegetables, stir well and lower the heat. Sauté the vegetables for 5–10 mins until they are soft.

8. Add the tomato purée, tinned tomatoes, stock, sugar (if using) and seasoning.

9. Bring the soup to the boil and then turn down to simmer for 15 mins.

10. Taste and add salt or pepper if needed.

11. Put the saucepan on a pot stand and blend the soup to a smooth consistency with a hand blender.

12. Serve in the soup tureen with your chosen garnish on top.

Evaluation

Date of Practical: _____

Q1. Personal Reflection: Did I ...?

Set up my unit correctly? ☐ ☐ ☐

Dice the vegetables evenly? ☐ ☐ ☐

Heat oil until hot? ☐ ☐ ☐

Sauté the vegetables until they began to soften? ☐ ☐ ☐

Use correct temperature control throughout? ☐ ☐ ☐

Blend the soup until smooth? ☐ ☐ ☐

Garnish the soup attractively? ☐ ☐ ☐

Have a well-flavoured end product? ☐ ☐ ☐

Keep a tidy and well-organised unit throughout? ☐ ☐ ☐

Prepare, serve and clean within the time available? ☐ ☐ ☐

Q2. Evaluate your dish using the following headings:

COLOUR _____

_____

FLAVOUR _____

_____

TEXTURE _____

_____

CRITICAL FRIEND _____

_____

Q3. Based on your evaluation of the colour, flavour and texture and the comments of your critical friend, identify any changes you would make to your tomato soup.

_____

_____

_____

_____

_____

_____

_____

_____

Q4. Identify a new skill you learned while making this dish. Evaluate how effectively you carried out this skill.

NEW SKILL _____

EFFECTIVENESS OF IMPLEMENTATION: _____

_____

_____

Q5. Optional activity: Homemade soup contributes many nutrients to the diet due to the use of numerous fresh vegetables, meat, starches, etc. Assess the nutritive and dietetic value of this soup in the diet.

Nutrient	Value in the diet

Q6. Optional activity: According to the Food Safety Authority of Ireland, consumption of salt in adults is 10 g per day. The Recommended Dietary Allowance (RDA) is 4 g per day. Commercial stock cubes and commercial soups can be a major contributor of salt to the diet.

(a) Working with your partner, carry out an investigation of the salt content of a variety of commercially available stock cubes and soups.

Food item	Brand	Salt content
Dried stock		
Organic stock		
Gel stock		
Dried soup		
Cook–chill soup		
Canned soup		

(b) Suggest two ways of reducing the salt content of homemade soup.

1. _____

2. _____

12 Movie Night Treat

Serves: 4   **45 mins**

Perfect dish for all class lengths.

Ingredients

1 packet tortilla chips (plain flavour is best)

100 g Cheddar cheese

1 carton sour cream

TO MAKE THE SALSA:
1 large tomato, ½ red onion, handful fresh coriander, salt and pepper

TO MAKE THE GUACAMOLE:
1 avocado, 1 clove garlic (optional), 1 lime, salt and pepper

Equipment

Chopping board(s) (colour-coded), sharp knife, garlic crusher, two small mixing bowls, grater, juicer, ovenproof dish, three small dip bowls, cutlery, two large plates (for cutlery).

Method

1. HANDS, APRON, EQUIPMENT and SET UP UNIT.

2. Preheat the grill to a high temperature.

3. *To make the salsa:* Wash the tomato, remove and discard the wood, slice and dice it.

4. Peel and dice the red onion.

5. Wash the coriander and chop it finely using the chiffonade technique.

6. Mix all the ingredients together and season with salt and pepper.

7. *To make the guacamole:* Peel and crush the garlic (if using).

8. Roll the lime on your workbench to make juicing easier, then halve and juice it.

9. Halve the avocado, remove the stone, scoop out the flesh and mash it with the garlic and lime juice using a fork. Season with salt and pepper.

10. Grate the cheese.

11. Pour the tortillas chips into a large ovenproof dish.

12. Sprinkle the grated cheese on top. Place under the grill and melt the cheese until it bubbles slightly.

13. Decant the salsa and guacamole into their own serving bowls, along with the sour cream as another serving dip. They can be placed on the side. Alternatively, pile the salsa, guacamole and sour cream attractively on top of the chips.

14. Sit back and enjoy the movie!

> **TOP TIP**
> A 'chiffonade' is a slicing technique where flat-leaved herbs such as coriander or leafy green vegetables such as spinach are cut into long, thin strips. You do this by stacking the leaves, rolling them tightly, then slicing the leaves perpendicular to the roll.

> **TOP TIP**
> When making guacamole it is essential to use a ripe avocado. A ripe avocado should feel soft but not mushy to the touch.

Evaluation

Date of Practical: _____

Q1. Personal Reflection: Did I ...?

Set up my unit correctly? ☐ ☐ ☐

Use my knife safely? ☐ ☐ ☐

Use the grater safely? ☐ ☐ ☐

Dice ingredients for the salsa finely? ☐ ☐ ☐

Finely chop the coriander using the chiffonade technique? ☐ ☐ ☐

Preheat the grill to correct temperature? ☐ ☐ ☐

Melt the cheese until it bubbled? ☐ ☐ ☐

Serve the dish attractively? ☐ ☐ ☐

Keep a tidy and well-organised unit throughout? ☐ ☐ ☐

Prepare, serve and clean within the time available? ☐ ☐ ☐

Q2. Evaluate your dish using the following headings:

COLOUR
_____
_____

FLAVOUR
_____
_____

TEXTURE
_____
_____

CRITICAL FRIEND
_____
_____

Q3. Based on your evaluation of the colour, flavour and texture and the comments of your critical friend, identify any changes you would make to your movie night treat.

_____

_____

_____

_____

Q4. List two guidelines to follow when using the grill for cooking.

GUIDELINE 1 _____

_____

GUIDELINE 2 _____

_____

Q5. Optional activity: Sour cream and avocados are ingredients that are high in fat. Not all fats are unhealthy, but fat should be eaten in moderation as part of a healthy diet. Find out how much fat is typically in a serving of sour cream and an avocado, the type of fat it is and the health implications of this fat in the diet.

Food	% content	Type of fat	Health implications
Sour cream			
Avocado			

Q6. Optional activity: An investigation of commercial guacamole dips found that the following list of additives (given in the table below) were used in their production. With your partner, classify the additives and assess their purpose in the guacamole.

Classifications

○ Colourings

○ Preservatives

○ Antioxidants

○ Flavourings and sweeteners

○ Nutritive additives

○ Physical conditioning agents

Additive	Classification	Purpose
Antioxidant		
Salt		
Acidity regulators		
Colours		
Xanthan gum		
Potassium sorbate		

UNIT 3
Home Baking

13. OAT BREAD

14. WHITE AND BROWN SODA BREAD

15. BANANA BREAD

16. COCONUT BUNS

17. SCONES – WHOLEMEAL/WHITE/ FRUIT/SAVOURY/ CITRUS/COCONUT

18. MUFFINS – LEMON AND POPPY SEED/BANANA/ CHOCOLATE CHIP/ BLUEBERRY

19. QUEEN CAKES

20. SIMPLE COOKIES

21. SPECIAL OCCASION CHOCOLATE FUDGE CAKE

22. FLAPJACKS

23. SPONGE WITH A TWIST

24. PASTRY – TO MAKE QUICHE/TART/ SAUSAGE ROLLS

13 Oat Bread

Learning Intentions

☆ Use nutritional knowledge to choose additional ingredients for the oat bread.

☆ Use a variety of preparation and cooking techniques to make this dish.

☆ Apply appropriate hygiene and safety rules when making this dish.

☆ Evaluate the sensory attributes of this dish and examine its contribution to a healthy diet.

Serves: 8–10   **1 hr**

For one-hour classes, use a loaf tin liner to save on wash-up. The bread can also be collected at lunch time.

Ingredients

1 large tub natural yogurt (500 ml)

1 tsp bread soda

1 egg

1 tbsp treacle

2 large tubs porridge oats (use empty yogurt tub to measure this)

50 g seeds/nuts/raisins/cheese, etc. (optional/to garnish)

Equipment

Mixing bowl, sieve, wooden spoon, metal spoon, loaf tin, pastry brush/loaf tin liner, oven gloves, wire tray, cutlery, two large plates (for cutlery).

Method

1. HANDS, APRON, EQUIPMENT and SET UP UNIT.

2. Preheat the oven to 190°C/gas mark 5.

3. Line the loaf tin with loaf tin liner or grease with a little oil using a pastry brush.

4. Empty the yogurt into the mixing bowl. Sieve in the bread soda. Add the egg and treacle and stir the mixture until it fizzes. This indicates that the raising agent has been activated.

5. Use the empty yogurt tub to measure the oats. Add the two tubs of oats and any optional ingredients and mix well.

6. Spoon the mixture into the loaf tin.

7. (If using) Sprinkle some seeds on top to garnish.

8. Place in the oven for 45 mins. The bread will darken on top.

9. Remove from the oven using oven gloves. Check for doneness by tapping on the bottom of the loaf – a hollow sound indicates doneness.

10. If done, leave to cool on a wire tray.

11. Serve in slices with your favourite topping.

TOP TIP

Loaf tin liners are very convenient when cooking this bread in school. Limited class time means that the bread can be removed at the end of class but the tin should remain clean!

TOP TIP

Using the yogurt container as a measuring tool makes this a great introduction to bread-making for younger members of the family.

Evaluation

Date of Practical: _____

Q1. Personal Reflection: Did I ...?

Set up my unit correctly? ☐ ☐ ☐

Preheat the oven to correct temperature? ☐ ☐ ☐

Measure my ingredients accurately? ☐ ☐ ☐

Stir the liquid ingredients until the raising agent was activated? ☐ ☐ ☐

Add and mix the dry ingredients thoroughly? ☐ ☐ ☐

Bake for the correct amount of time? ☐ ☐ ☐

Remove safely from the loaf tin? ☐ ☐ ☐

Test for doneness correctly? ☐ ☐ ☐

Keep a tidy and well-organised unit throughout? ☐ ☐ ☐

Prepare, serve and clean within the time available? ☐ ☐ ☐

Q2. Evaluate your dish using the following headings:

COLOUR _____

_____

FLAVOUR _____

_____

TEXTURE _____

_____

CRITICAL FRIEND _____

_____

Q3. Based on your evaluation of the colour, flavour and texture and the comments of your critical friend, identify any changes you would make to your oat bread.

_____
_____
_____
_____
_____
_____
_____
_____

Q5. Optional activity: Identify two changes that could be made to this recipe to modify it for the following diets.

Diet	Modification
Coeliac	
Lactose intolerance	

Q4. Baking is often associated with breads and cakes. List other foods that can be cooked by baking.

_____
_____
_____
_____

Q6. Optional activity: Oats are often used in recipes as part of a balanced, varied diet. In pairs, research one of the following topics. Prepare a short summary of your research for the rest of the class.

List some novel uses for oats.	List five nutritious ways to serve porridge.
Explain: What are 'overnight oats' and how are they made?	Are organic oats more nutritious than non-organic oats? Explain your answer.
Investigate the nutritional value of oats.	Investigate whether or not a diet rich in oats can help with weight loss.
Investigate whether or not oats are suitable for coeliacs.	Oats are a 'low GI' food. Investigate this term.

14 White and Brown Soda Bread

Serves: Many!

50 mins

Perfect dish for all class lengths.

Learning Intentions

☆ Demonstrate the correct culinary techniques required to prepare and cook this dish.

☆ Apply appropriate hygiene and safety rules when making this dish.

☆ Evaluate the sensory attributes of this dish and examine its contribution to a healthy diet.

☆ Compare the nutritional benefits of white soda bread and brown soda bread.

White Soda Bread

Ingredients

400 g plain white flour

½ tsp salt

½ tsp bread soda

300 ml buttermilk

Equipment

Weighing scales, mixing bowl, sieve, measuring jug, wooden spoon, flour dredger, baking tray, knife, pastry brush, oven gloves, wire tray, cutlery, two large plates (for cutlery).

Method

1. HANDS, APRON, EQUIPMENT and SET UP UNIT.

2. Preheat the oven to 180°C/gas mark 4.

3. Weigh the flour and measure the salt, bread soda and buttermilk.

4. Sieve the flour, salt and bread soda high over a bowl. Sieving the ingredients from a height will encourage air into the mixture, adding to the lightness of the dough.

5. Add most of the milk and mix it well. Add the remainder of the milk (if needed) in small amounts until you have a slightly sticky dough.

6. Dredge flour onto the table and knead the dough until smooth on one side.

7. Turn the smooth side up. Flatten and shape it into a circle.

8. Place it on a floured baking tray. Cut a cross on top and brush with a little milk.

9. Bake in the oven for 30–35 mins. Remove from the oven using oven gloves and test for doneness by tapping the bottom (a hollow sound indicates doneness). The bread should also be golden brown in colour.

10. If done, set to cool on a wire tray.

11. Serve when cooled.

Brown Soda Bread

Ingredients

360 g coarse wholemeal flour

30 g wheat bran

150 g plain white flour

½ tsp salt

1 tsp bread soda

400 ml buttermilk

Equipment

As with white soda bread list.

Method

Follow the same method as for white soda bread. Add the wholemeal flour and wheat bran with the plain flour at Step 4.

TOP TIP

Home bakers possess a wealth of knowledge and skill from their years of experience, often adding their own twists or techniques to recipes. These soda bread recipes and methods come from a wonderful cook called Mary Hyland, from Fermoy in Co. Cork. It is important to learn how to bake and cook healthy, nourishing meals from those around us who possess these important skills. It can also be a valuable way of spending time with people who are important to us.

Evaluation

Date of Practical: _____

Q1. Personal Reflection: Did I ...?

Set up my unit correctly? ☐ ☐ ☐

Weigh and measure ingredients accurately? ☐ ☐ ☐

Preheat the oven to correct temperature? ☐ ☐ ☐

Sieve ingredients high over the bowl? ☐ ☐ ☐

Add ingredients in the correct order? ☐ ☐ ☐

Use oven gloves when taking my bread out of the oven? ☐ ☐ ☐

Check the bread had a hollow sound when tapped underneath to ensure it was baked? ☐ ☐ ☐

Observe the colour of the bread to ensure it was baked? ☐ ☐ ☐

Have a well-flavoured end product? ☐ ☐ ☐

Have a well-risen bread? ☐ ☐ ☐

Keep a tidy and well-organised unit throughout? ☐ ☐ ☐

Prepare, serve and clean within the time available? ☐ ☐ ☐

Q2. Evaluate your dish using the following headings:

COLOUR _____

_____

FLAVOUR _____

_____

TEXTURE _____

_____

CRITICAL FRIEND _____

_____

Q3. Based on your evaluation of the colour, flavour and texture and the comments of your critical friend, identify any changes you would make to your soda bread.

_____

_____

_____

_____

_____

_____

Q4. Why is it important to avoid opening the oven door unnecessarily while baking?

_____

_____

Explain briefly the purpose of kneading.

_____

_____

Q5. Optional activity: Brown soda bread is a healthier option than white soda bread. In the box below, identify two nutritional differences between the two types of breads.

Nutritional differences between white and brown soda bread
1.
2.

Q6. Optional activity: In small groups, research one of the following topics. Prepare a short summary of your research for the rest of the class.

List the advantages and disadvantages of home baking.	What is a raising agent? State the different types of raising agents available. Explain briefly how one works.	Describe a way to check that each of the following is baked: bread; cakes; sponges.
Identify and explain the different types of flour available to buy in our supermarkets.	Compile a set of rules to follow when home baking.	Name and briefly explain the different methods of cake-making. Include examples of baked-product recipes that use the stated cake-making method.

15 Banana Bread

Learning Intentions

☆ Demonstrate the correct culinary techniques required to prepare and cook this dish.

☆ Apply appropriate hygiene and safety rules when making this dish.

☆ Evaluate the sensory attributes of this dish and examine its contribution to a healthy diet.

☆ Discuss the contribution banana bread can make to food sustainability.

Serves: Many!   **1 hr 10 mins**

For one-hour classes, use a loaf tin liner to save on wash-up. The bread can also be collected at lunch time.

Ingredients

80 ml vegetable/coconut oil

225 g self-raising flour

½ tsp salt

½ tsp nutmeg

½ tsp cinnamon

50 g caster sugar

50 g light brown sugar

1 egg

1 tbsp treacle

½ tsp vanilla extract/essence

4 ripe bananas

OPTIONAL:
50 g chopped walnuts/
50 g chocolate chips

Equipment

Chopping board(s) (colour-coded), sharp knife, weighing scales, large mixing bowl, sieve, measuring jug, wooden spoon, fork, large plate, loaf tin, loaf tin liner, pastry brush, spatula, skewer, oven gloves, wire tray, cutlery, two large plates (for cutlery).

Method

1. HANDS, APRON, EQUIPMENT and SET UP UNIT.

2. Preheat the oven to 180°C/gas mark 4.

3. Weigh and measure all ingredients. Line the loaf tin with a loaf tin liner or grease with a little oil using a pastry brush.

4. If using coconut oil, melt it over a gentle heat and leave to cool.

5. Sieve the flour, salt, nutmeg and cinnamon into a large mixing bowl. Add the caster sugar and light brown sugar and stir.

6. In a measuring jug, mix the egg, vegetable oil/cooled coconut oil, treacle and vanilla extract together. Stir this wet mixture into the flour.

7. Using a fork, mash the bananas on a large plate or in a bowl. If using walnuts, chop roughly.

8. Add the bananas and walnuts/chocolate chips into the mixture. Stir in gently.

9. Pour the mixture into the loaf tin, scraping the bowl down with the spatula. Place in the oven for 50 mins. Test with a skewer for doneness – it should be dry and clean when removed from the banana bread. The bread should be a golden brown colour.

10. If done, remove from the oven using oven gloves. Leave in tin to cool and then remove to a wire tray.

11. Serve and enjoy!

TOP TIP

Using well-ripened bananas will add to the overall flavour and success of the dish. A loaf of banana bread is also an excellent way of helping to reduce and avoid food waste in the home by using up these well-ripened bananas that might otherwise be left to rot.

Evaluation

Date of Practical: _____

Q1. Personal Reflection: Did I ...?

Set up my unit correctly? ☐ ☐ ☐

Weigh and measure ingredients accurately? ☐ ☐ ☐

Preheat the oven to correct temperature? ☐ ☐ ☐

Add ingredients in the correct order? ☐ ☐ ☐

Stir the wet ingredients into the dry ingredients? ☐ ☐ ☐

Bake for the correct length of time? ☐ ☐ ☐

Test for doneness correctly? ☐ ☐ ☐

Have a well-flavoured end product? ☐ ☐ ☐

Keep a tidy and well-organised unit throughout? ☐ ☐ ☐

Prepare, serve and clean within the time available? ☐ ☐ ☐

Q2. Evaluate your dish using the following headings:

COLOUR _____

_____

FLAVOUR _____

_____

TEXTURE _____

_____

CRITICAL FRIEND _____

_____

Q3. Based on your evaluation of the colour, flavour and texture and the comments of your critical friend, identify any changes you would make to your banana bread.

_____

_____

_____

_____

_____

_____

_____

Q4. Name the raising agent(s) used in this recipe. Give two reasons why raising agents are used in baking.

Raising agent: _____

Reason 1: _____

_____

Reason 2: _____

_____

Q5. Optional activity: **Coconut oil can be used in this banana bread recipe. Identify two benefits of using coconut oil. Name another type of oil that could be used in this recipe as an alternative to coconut oil.**

Benefit 1: _____

_____

Benefit 2: _____

_____

Alternate oil: _____

Q6. Optional activity: To check that banana bread is baked, a skewer is inserted and if it comes out clean this establishes that the bread is cooked. With your partner, discuss and note in your copy how you would identify that the following products were baked: sponge cake; apple crumble; quiche; brown soda bread; blueberry muffins.

16 Coconut Buns

Makes: 8–10 buns

50 mins

Perfect dish for all class lengths.

Ingredients

200 g self-raising flour

¼ tsp salt

75 g margarine/butter

75 g sugar

50 g desiccated coconut

1 egg

100 ml milk

TO DECORATE:

jam and desiccated coconut

TOP TIP

If you do not have self-raising flour, use 200 g of plain flour along with 1 tsp of baking powder.

Equipment

Weighing scales, sieve, mixing bowl, wooden spoon, measuring jug, baking tray/patty tin, oven gloves, wire tray, small bowl, plate, cutlery, two large plates (for cutlery).

Method

1. HANDS, APRON, EQUIPMENT and SET UP UNIT.
2. Preheat the oven to 200ºC/gas mark 6.
3. Weigh and measure all ingredients.
4. Sieve the flour and salt into the mixing bowl.
5. Rub in margarine/butter using fingertips until it resembles breadcrumbs.
6. Stir in the sugar and coconut.
7. Crack the egg into a measuring jug and mix together with the milk.
8. Add half of this liquid to the flour mixture and stir well. Add the rest of the liquid slowly, a little at a time, to make a stiff dough.
9. Prepare the baking tray by flouring it or greasing it with a little margarine. Alternatively, use a patty tin lightly greased with a little margarine.
10. Using two forks/spoons, make 8 to 10 buns on the baking tray/in the patty tin.
11. Bake for 15 mins. Check one for doneness by tapping on the bottom (there should be a hollow sound). The buns should also be golden brown in colour.
12. If done, remove from the oven using oven gloves. Remove each bun to the wire tray to cool.
13. Soften the jam by beating it in a small bowl. Place the coconut on a plate.
14. Dip the top of the buns into the jam and then into the coconut to decorate.
15. Serve on a plate with a doily.

Evaluation

Date of Practical: _____

Q1. Personal Reflection: Did I ...?

Set up my unit correctly? ☐ ☐ ☐

Weigh and measure ingredients accurately? ☐ ☐ ☐

Preheat the oven to correct temperature? ☐ ☐ ☐

Rub the margarine into the flour until it resembled breadcrumbs? ☐ ☐ ☐

Mix the egg and milk together in a jug? ☐ ☐ ☐

Stir in the egg and milk mixture as directed? ☐ ☐ ☐

Form 8–10 coconut buns on a baking tray or in a patty tin and bake until browned? ☐ ☐ ☐

Soften jam in a small bowl and dip the buns in the softened jam and then into the coconut? ☐ ☐ ☐

Serve the buns attractively? ☐ ☐ ☐

Have a well-flavoured end product? ☐ ☐ ☐

Keep a tidy and well-organised unit throughout? ☐ ☐ ☐

Prepare, serve and clean within the time available? ☐ ☐ ☐

Q2. Evaluate your dish using the following headings:

COLOUR _____

_____

FLAVOUR _____

_____

TEXTURE _____

_____

CRITICAL FRIEND _____

_____

Q3. Based on your evaluation of the colour, flavour and texture and the comments of your critical friend, identify any changes you would make to your coconut buns.

Q4. Baking is the cooking method used in this recipe. Explain why it is important to preheat the oven before baking.

Q5. Optional activity: The skill of modifying recipes is an essential component of Home Economics. Identify two modifications you could make to the ingredients list to help keep the dish in line with Healthy Eating Guidelines.

Healthy Eating Guideline	Modification
1.	
2.	

Q6. Optional activity:
A knowledge of how food cooks is an essential component of understanding cookery.

(a) In your copy, list three methods of heat transfer.

(b) Explain each of these methods.

(c) Give examples of dishes where these methods of heat transfer are used in the cooking of the dish.

17 Scones

Makes: 10–12 scones

50 mins

(depending on size of cutter)

Perfect dish for all class lengths.

Ingredients

WHOLEMEAL SCONES

250 g self-raising flour

250 g coarse wholemeal flour

1 tsp baking powder

pinch salt

50 g caster sugar

100 g margarine/butter

1 egg

300 ml milk

WHITE SCONES

450 g plain flour

85 g caster sugar

1 heaped tbsp baking powder

pinch salt

115 g margarine/butter

60 g natural yogurt

1 egg

170 ml milk

TO DECORATE/SERVE:

sesame/poppy seeds

butter/jam/cream

Variations

○ *Fruit scones:* Add 50 g dried raisins, sultanas or cherries to either mixture before adding the liquid.

○ *Savoury scones:* Add 50 g cheese to the wholemeal recipe before adding the liquid. A teaspoon of dried chives/wholegrain mustard/paprika/4 olives/4 sundried tomatoes could also be added to complement the cheese.

○ *Citrus scones:* Add zest of 1 lemon/orange to the white scone recipe before rubbing in the margarine.

○ *Coconut scones:* Add 50 g desiccated coconut with the sugar to the white scone recipe.

Equipment

Weighing scales, mixing bowl, wooden spoon, measuring jug, sieve, flour dredger, scone cutter, baking tray, pastry brush, oven gloves, wire tray, cutlery, two large plates (for cutlery).

Method

1. HANDS, APRON, EQUIPMENT and SET UP UNIT.

2. Preheat the oven to 190°C/gas mark 5.

3. Weigh and measure all ingredients.

4. Sieve the flour (not wholemeal), baking powder and salt into the mixing bowl.

5. Rub in margarine/butter using fingertips until it resembles breadcrumbs. Stir in sugar (if using).

6. Crack the egg into the milk in a measuring jug and mix gently with a fork. (Add the yogurt at this point if making white scones.)

7. Add sufficient liquid to make a soft (not sticky) dough.

8. Turn onto a floured board and gently knead to remove any cracks.

9. Flatten out slightly to 3 cm in thickness, then cut out the scones using the cutter (quantity depends on size of cutter).

10. Place on a floured baking tray and glaze with any remaining liquid using a pastry brush. (For some scones, garnish can be added at this point, e.g. seeds or grated cheese.)

11. Bake for 15–20 mins until golden brown on top and on bottom. Check for doneness by tapping the bottom of the scones.

12. Remove from the oven using oven gloves to a wire tray for cooling.

13. Serve with butter and jam or cream, etc.

TOP TIP

Dip the scone cutter into some flour before cutting out the scones. This prevents the mixture sticking to the cutter and will give a neat, sharp edge to the cooked scone.

Evaluation

Date of Practical: _____

Q1. Personal Reflection: Did I ...?

Set up my unit correctly? ☐ ☐ ☐

Weigh and measure ingredients accurately? ☐ ☐ ☐

Preheat the oven to correct temperature? ☐ ☐ ☐

Rub the margarine into the flour until it resembled breadcrumbs? ☐ ☐ ☐

Add the correct amount of liquid? ☐ ☐ ☐

Knead the dough gently? ☐ ☐ ☐

Cut out the scones evenly using a cutter and glaze them? ☐ ☐ ☐

Bake for the correct amount of time? ☐ ☐ ☐

Test for doneness correctly? ☐ ☐ ☐

Cool the scones on a wire tray? ☐ ☐ ☐

Keep a tidy and well-organised unit throughout? ☐ ☐ ☐

Prepare, serve and clean within the time available? ☐ ☐ ☐

Q2. Evaluate your dish using the following headings:

COLOUR
_____
_____

FLAVOUR
_____
_____

TEXTURE
_____
_____

CRITICAL FRIEND
_____
_____

Q3. Based on your evaluation of the colour, flavour and texture and the comments of your critical friend, identify any changes you would make to your scones.

_____

_____

_____

_____

Q4. Scones are made using the rubbing-in method. Outline two guidelines you should follow when using this method of baking.

1: _____

_____

2: _____

_____

Q5. Optional activity: Referring to the ingredients list, identify how any of the scones recipes could be modified to make them suitable for these two specific diets.

Diet	Modifications
Active teenager	
Coeliac	

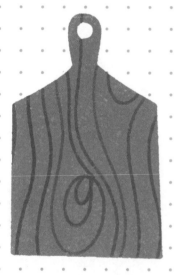

Q6. Optional activity: As a class, brainstorm the different flours that could be used to make scones. Then in groups of four, choose one flour from the brainstormed list and carry out these activities:

(a) Name the cereal from which this flour is extracted.

(b) Find a picture of the cereal plant as it grows in the field.

(c) Identify the part(s) of the cereal grain used to make the flour you are investigating.

(d) Name dishes that could be made using this flour.

Present your group's findings to the rest of the class and discuss.

18 Muffins

Makes: 9 large muffins

50 mins

Note that there may not be enough time in a one-hour class to complete lemon and poppy seed muffins.

Learning Intentions

☆ Demonstrate the correct culinary techniques required to prepare and cook this dish.

☆ Apply appropriate hygiene and safety rules when making this dish.

☆ Evaluate the sensory attributes of this dish and examine its contribution to a healthy diet.

Ingredients

CHOCOLATE CHIP MUFFINS

125 g margarine/butter

250 g self-raising flour

1 tsp baking powder

½ tsp bread soda

125 g caster sugar

1 tbsp cocoa powder

100 g chocolate chips

1 large egg

150 ml milk

½ tsp vanilla essence

Ingredients

LEMON AND POPPY SEED MUFFINS

115 g butter

280 g plain flour

2 tsp baking powder

½ tsp bread soda

130 g sugar

1 ½ tbsp poppy seeds

2 medium eggs

75 ml milk

½ tsp vanilla essence/ extract

fresh juice from 2 lemons

grated zest from 2 lemons

3 tsp lemon essence/ lemon curd

125 g natural/lemon yogurt

Ingredients

BANANA MUFFINS

75 g butter

250 g self-raising flour

1 tsp baking powder

½ tsp bread soda

½ tsp ground cinnamon

½ tsp ground nutmeg

115 g caster sugar

2 eggs

125 ml milk

1 tsp vanilla essence

2 large overripe bananas with black spots

Ingredients

BLUEBERRY MUFFINS

250 g self-raising flour

150 g caster sugar

1 heaped tsp baking powder

1 large egg

150 ml milk

½ tsp vanilla essence or vanilla extract

125 g butter/margarine

125 g blueberries

Equipment

Bun cases, muffin tray, saucepan, measuring jug, mixing bowl, sieve, spatula, wooden spoon, two tablespoons, skewer, oven gloves, wire tray, serving plate, cutlery, two large plates (for cutlery).

Method

1. HANDS, APRON, EQUIPMENT and SET UP UNIT.

2. Preheat the oven to 180°C/gas mark 4.

3. Weigh and measure all ingredients.

4. Put the cases into the muffin tray.

5. Melt the margarine/butter on the hob and allow it to cool.

6. Sieve the flour, baking powder and bread soda high over a large bowl. Sieving the ingredients from a height will encourage air into the mixture, adding to the lightness of the dough.

7. Stir in all the remaining dry ingredients from your recipe.

8. Mix the egg, milk and vanilla essence into the cooled margarine/butter. Stir in any remaining wet ingredients from your recipe.

9. Add the wet ingredients to the dry ingredients and stir together to form a soft mixture. If making blueberry muffins, gently fold the blueberries through at this point. Do not overmix.

10. Using two tablespoons, spoon the mixture into the muffin cases until approximately ⅔ full.

11. Bake for 20–25 mins until golden brown and cooked through. Test for doneness using a skewer.

12. Remove from the oven using oven gloves. Remove from the muffin tray to a wire tray and allow to cool.

13. To serve, sprinkle with icing sugar.

TOP TIP

Do not over-stir or overbeat the muffin mixture. It is important to just moisten the ingredients and stir gently. The final mixture should be thick. The reason for this is to avoid knocking out any additional air that has been gained during the sieving process. Well-risen and aerated muffins are key to a successful muffin bake.

TOP TIP

There are many different types of muffins that can be made. They are an easy way of adding extra fruit to our diet. Blueberry and raspberry muffins are examples of popular fruit muffins.

Evaluation

Date of Practical: _____

Q1. Personal Reflection: Did I ...?

Set up my unit correctly? ☐ ☐ ☐

Weigh and measure ingredients accurately? ☐ ☐ ☐

Preheat the oven to correct temperature? ☐ ☐ ☐

Add the wet ingredients to the dry ingredients and stir together to form a soft mixture? ☐ ☐ ☐

Spoon the mixture into each muffin case until approx. ⅔ full? ☐ ☐ ☐

Bake for the correct amount of time? ☐ ☐ ☐

Test for doneness correctly? ☐ ☐ ☐

Have a well-flavoured end product? ☐ ☐ ☐

Keep a tidy and well-organised unit throughout? ☐ ☐ ☐

Prepare, serve and clean within the time available? ☐ ☐ ☐

Q2. Evaluate your dish using the following headings:

COLOUR _____

_____

FLAVOUR _____

_____

TEXTURE _____

_____

CRITICAL FRIEND _____

_____

Q3. Based on your evaluation of the colour, flavour and texture and the comments of your critical friend, identify any changes you would make to your muffins.

_____

_____

_____

_____

_____

_____

_____

Q4. When baking, why is it important to weigh and measure ingredients accurately?

_____

_____

Q5. Optional activity: In your opinion, which of the four muffin recipes is closest to keeping in line with Healthy Eating Guidelines. Give two reasons for your answer.

Chosen muffin:	
Reason 1:	
Reason 2:	

Q6. Optional activity: As a class, complete a sensory comparison between a shop-bought muffin and a homemade muffin. Buy one muffin of a similar variety to the one you are making in class. Then compare the muffins using the following headings:

Compare	Homemade muffin	Shop-bought muffin
Colour		
Taste		
Texture		
Cost per 100 g (use the costing template on p. 187)		
Any other notes		

19 Queen Cakes

Equipment

Bun cases, bun tray, measuring jug, fork, sieve, plate, electric mixer, mixing bowl, whisk, two tablespoons, skewer, oven gloves, wire tray, cupcake stand/serving plate, cutlery, two large plates (for cutlery).

Method

TOP TIP

The 'two-spoon method' mentioned in Step 11 is a technique for transferring mixture from a bowl into a paper case or onto a baking sheet. Load one spoon with the mixture and use the second spoon in the other hand to push the mixture off the spoon into the case/onto the tray.

1. HANDS, APRON, EQUIPMENT and SET UP UNIT.

2. Preheat the oven to 180°C/gas mark 4.

3. Weigh and measure all ingredients.

4. Put bun cases into the bun tray.

5. Crack both eggs into a measuring jug or cup. Gently beat the eggs using a fork.

6. Sieve the flour onto a plate and set aside.

7. Using an electric beater on a low setting, mix the margarine and sugar together for approximately 5 mins until pale and creamy.

8. Add half the egg and half the flour to the creamed mixture and whisk gently until combined.

9. Add the remaining egg and vanilla essence. Beat for one minute.

10. Gently fold in the remaining flour until well combined.

11. Using two tablespoons, fill each bun case until approximately ⅔ full (the two-spoon method).

12. Wipe up any spills on the bun tray before placing in the oven.

13. Bake for 15 mins until golden brown. Test with a skewer.

14. Remove from the oven using oven gloves, remove from the bun tray to a wire tray and allow to cool.

15. Decorate the buns as you like (see 'Decorating options' below).

16. Serve on a cupcake stand or on an attractive plate.

Learning Intentions

☆ Demonstrate the correct culinary techniques required to prepare and cook this dish.

☆ Apply appropriate hygiene and safety rules when making this dish.

☆ Demonstrate culinary skills in making an attractive icing for the queen cakes.

☆ Evaluate the sensory attributes of this dish and examine its contribution to a healthy diet.

Makes: 10–12 buns   1 hr

In a one-hour class, these buns can be decorated quickly using melted chocolate and sprinkles.

Ingredients

2 eggs

150 g self-raising flour (alternatively use 150 g plain flour and ½ tsp baking powder)

100 g margarine

100 g caster sugar

2 drops vanilla essence

Decorating options

○ *Butter icing ingredients:* 200 g icing sugar, 100 g butter/margarine , 1–2 tbsp water. Optional: a few drops of colouring and/or a few drops of vanilla essence or almond essence for flavour.
  Method: Cream butter/margarine, add sieved icing sugar and beat until soft. Add water, if needed, until the icing is soft enough to pipe.. Beat in chosen colouring/flavouring. Pipe on using a piping bag. Add sprinkles.

○ *Chocolate decoration:* Melt cooking chocolate and coat the top of the bun with it. Add jellies, buttons, sprinkles, etc.

○ *White icing decoration:* Add a little boiled water to sieved icing sugar. Stir and beat until it forms a thick white icing paste. To colour, add a few drops of food colouring. Coat the top of the bun with the icing. Add jellies, buttons, sprinkles, etc.

Evaluation

Date of Practical: _____

Q1. Personal Reflection: Did I ....?

Set up my unit correctly? ☐ ☐ ☐

Weigh and measure ingredients accurately? ☐ ☐ ☐

Preheat the oven to correct temperature? ☐ ☐ ☐

Cream the butter and sugar until pale and creamy? ☐ ☐ ☐

Add the ingredients in the correct order? ☐ ☐ ☐

Use the two-spoon method to evenly divide the mixture into each of the bun cases? ☐ ☐ ☐

Bake for the correct length of time? ☐ ☐ ☐

Test for doneness correctly? ☐ ☐ ☐

Cool the queen cakes on a wire tray and decorate attractively? ☐ ☐ ☐

Have a well-flavoured end product? ☐ ☐ ☐

Keep a tidy and well-organised unit throughout? ☐ ☐ ☐

Prepare, serve and clean within the time available? ☐ ☐ ☐

Q2. Evaluate your dish using the following headings:

COLOUR _____

_____

FLAVOUR _____

_____

TEXTURE _____

_____

CRITICAL FRIEND _____

_____

Q3. Based on your evaluation of the colour, flavour and texture and the comments of your critical friend, identify any changes you would make to your queen cakes.

Q4. Queen cakes are made using the creaming method. Explain how this method is carried out.

Q5. Optional activity: Identify modifications you would make to the ingredients list to suit the following two specific diets:

Diet	Modifications
Coeliac	
Diabetic type 2	

Q6. Optional activity: In groups of three, design a creative way of icing or decorating a queen cake. You must choose a theme or a particular occasion. Use the internet or cookery books for inspiration. Present a picture of your chosen queen cake design to your class with the theme or occasion identified.

20 Simple Cookies

Makes: 8 large-/12 medium-sized cookies

1 hr

In a one-hour class, either shorten the length of time to chill the dough, or eliminate this step. Also make sure to use the top and bottom ovens to maximise space when making this dish.

Ingredients

190 g plain flour

½ tsp salt

½ tsp baking soda

1 large egg

1 tbsp milk

1 tsp vanilla extract/ essence

110 g butter

30 g caster sugar

110 g light brown sugar

150 g milk/dark chocolate chips/75 g chopped hazelnuts and 75 g chocolate chips

TOP TIP

It is better to chill the cookie dough before cooking, as this results in a more solid cookie mixture and an enhanced flavour.

Equipment

Baking tray, greaseproof paper, sieve, plate, small metal or glass bowl, whisk, mixing bowl, electric hand mixer or a stand mixer, wooden spoon, ice cream scoop/tablespoon, oven gloves, wire tray, cutlery, two large plates (for cutlery).

Method

1. HANDS, APRON, EQUIPMENT and SET UP UNIT.

2. Preheat the oven to 180°C/gas mark 4.

3. Weigh and measure all ingredients.

4. Line a large baking tray with greaseproof paper.

5. Sieve the flour, salt and baking soda onto a plate and set aside.

6. In a metal or glass bowl, whisk the egg, milk and vanilla extract together.

7. In another mixing bowl or stand mixer, beat the butter and sugar together for approximately 2–3 mins until pale and creamy.

8. To this mixture add the egg, milk and vanilla extract mixture and combine all on a low setting for 30 secs.

9. Gradually add the flour and allow the ingredients to combine. Once this is done, stop mixing.

10. (If using) Add the chocolate chips (or hazelnuts and chocolate chips) and stir the mixture gently with a wooden spoon until they are evenly distributed.

11. (If possible) Chill the dough for a period of time.

12. Scoop the dough using an ice cream scoop onto the pre-lined baking sheet and gently flatten with the back of a spoon. Alternatively, roll a tablespoon of the dough into a ball and flatten. Leave plenty of space between each cookie. You can decide how big you want the cookies to be.

13. Bake for 14–15 mins in the middle of the oven until the cookies are a golden brown colour.

14. Remove from the oven using oven gloves and allow to cool for 5 mins before sliding the greaseproof paper onto a wire tray.

15. Allow to cool for a further 10 mins before serving.

Evaluation

Date of Practical: _____

Q1. Personal Reflection: Did I ...?

Set up my unit correctly? ☐ ☐ ☐

Weigh and measure ingredients accurately? ☐ ☐ ☐

Preheat the oven to correct temperature? ☐ ☐ ☐

Beat the butter and sugar until pale and creamy? ☐ ☐ ☐

Add the ingredients in the correct order? ☐ ☐ ☐

Combine all ingredients together? ☐ ☐ ☐

(If possible) Chill the dough for a period of time? ☐ ☐ ☐

Bake for the correct length of time? ☐ ☐ ☐

Test for doneness correctly? ☐ ☐ ☐

Have a well-flavoured end product? ☐ ☐ ☐

Keep a tidy and well-organised unit throughout? ☐ ☐ ☐

Prepare, serve and clean within the time available? ☐ ☐ ☐

Q2. Evaluate your dish using the following headings:

COLOUR
_____
_____

FLAVOUR
_____
_____

TEXTURE
_____
_____

CRITICAL FRIEND
_____
_____

Q3. Based on your evaluation of the colour, flavour and texture and the comments of your critical friend, identify any changes you would make to your cookies.

_____

_____

_____

_____

_____

_____

_____

Q4. State two advantages of chilling the cookie dough before baking it.

Advantage 1: _____

_____

Advantage 2: _____

_____

Q5. Optional activity: Cookies can be made using gluten-free flour. Draw the symbol found on gluten-free products. Then compare the price of gluten-free flour and plain flour per 100 g.

Gluten-free symbol:	Price comparison of gluten-free and plain flour per 100 g:	
	Gluten-free €	**Plain flour €**

Q6. Optional activity: Today, home-baking mixes such as Betty Crocker are very popular. In groups of three, nominate a different person for each of the following roles:

○ Note-keeper: Record the group's opinions.

○ Reporter: Report the findings of the group back to the rest of the class.

○ Time-keeper: Keep time.

Now discuss these questions in your group:

(a) Explain what baking mixes are.

(b) Give the advantages of cake mixes.

(c) Give the disadvantages of cake mixes.

(d) Which would you choose and why: (i) to make cookies/cake/bread from scratch; or (ii) to use the convenience mix?

21 Special Occasion Chocolate Fudge Cake

Serves: 10–12   55 mins

In a one-hour class, spreading chocolate spread onto the warm cake works well. If your class is longer, make buttercream icing or whip some cream and add it to the cooled cake.

Ingredients

FOR THE CAKE:

225 g soft butter

225 g sugar

5 eggs

100 g self-raising flour

250 g drinking chocolate

FOR THE ICING:

chocolate spread/ butter icing (see Recipe 19)/200 ml single cream (whipped)

TOP TIP

This is the perfect cake for a special occasion such as a birthday or even Easter. Research some novel decorating ideas and experiment at home for the next special day!

Equipment

Weighing scales, greaseproof paper, scissors, pastry brush, mixing bowl, sieve, electric whisk/food mixer, spatula, two 8" cake tins, oven gloves, wire tray, cutlery, two large plates (for cutlery).

Method

1. HANDS, APRON, EQUIPMENT and SET UP UNIT.

2. Preheat the oven to 190°C/gas mark 5.

3. Weigh and measure all ingredients.

4. Grease the base and sides of the tins with oil/butter. Cut circles of greaseproof paper and line the base of each tin.

5. Put the softened butter, sugar and eggs in the mixing bowl. Sieve in the flour and drinking chocolate. This is known as the all-in-one method.

6. Using the whisk, mix the ingredients thoroughly. Use a low speed at first until the ingredients are combined and then increase the speed.

7. Scrape the bowl down with the spatula and then give another brief mix.

8. Divide the cake mixture into the tins and cook for 25 mins.

9. When cooked the cake will have a slight wobble in the middle.

10. Remove from the oven using oven gloves. Cool the cakes in the tins for 10 mins and then turn onto a wire tray to cool fully.

11. Decorate the cake.

TOP TIP

The texture of this cake is similar to a brownie. Due to this and the small quantity of flour used in this recipe, this is an ideal cake to make for a coeliac with gluten-free flour.

Evaluation

Date of Practical: _____

Q1. Personal Reflection: Did I ...?

Set up my unit correctly? ☐ ☐ ☐

Weigh and measure ingredients accurately? ☐ ☐ ☐

Preheat the oven to correct temperature? ☐ ☐ ☐

Line the base of the tin correctly? ☐ ☐ ☐

Use the all-in-one method to make the cake? ☐ ☐ ☐

Mix until ingredients were evenly combined? ☐ ☐ ☐

Cook until there was still a wobble remaining? ☐ ☐ ☐

Cool fully before decorating? ☐ ☐ ☐

Decorate my dish attractively to suit a special occasion? ☐ ☐ ☐

Have a well-flavoured end product? ☐ ☐ ☐

Keep a tidy and well-organised unit throughout? ☐ ☐ ☐

Prepare, serve and clean within the time available? ☐ ☐ ☐

Q2. Evaluate your dish using the following headings:

COLOUR _____
_____

FLAVOUR _____
_____

TEXTURE _____
_____

CRITICAL FRIEND _____
_____

Q3. Based on your evaluation of the colour, flavour and texture and the comments of your critical friend, identify any changes you would make to your chocolate fudge cake.

_____

_____

_____

_____

_____

_____

_____

_____

Q4. This cake uses the all-in-one method. List one advantage and one disadvantage of using this method for making cakes.

ADVANTAGE _____

_____

_____

DISADVANTAGE _____

_____

_____

Q5. Optional activity: Every family has many special occasions to celebrate. This chocolate cake is the perfect cake for any of these occasions. Choose a special occasion and list healthy, savoury food options that can be served at this occasion also.

Chosen occasion:

_____

_____

_____

_____

_____

Q6. Optional activity: Design and draw your decorative idea for your special occasion chocolate cake. You can use any icing, but consider your own culinary skills to ensure the cake is achievable for you at home.

22 Flapjacks

Serves: 8–10

45 mins

plus extra for cooling

In a one-hour class, the flapjacks will have to be collected later. Bring your own baking tin to save time at the end.

Ingredients

125 g margarine/butter

125 g brown demerara sugar

75 g golden syrup/honey

225 g porridge oats

OPTIONAL EXTRAS (MORE THAN ONE CAN BE CHOSEN):

4 large dried apricots; 35 g desiccated coconut; 40 g raisins; 35 g walnuts/pecans; 35 g seeds

TO DECORATE (OPTIONAL):

50 g melted chocolate/crushed Crunchie bar

Equipment

Weighing scales, bowls, wooden spoon, saucepan, metal spoon, 8" baking tin, greaseproof paper, oven gloves, cutlery, two large plates (for cutlery).

Method

1. HANDS, APRON, EQUIPMENT and SET UP UNIT.

2. Preheat the oven to 180°C/gas mark 4.

3. Weigh and measure all ingredients into separate bowls.

4. Grease and line the baking tin with greaseproof paper.

5. Melt the margarine/butter with the sugar and syrup/honey in a saucepan on a medium heat.

6. Remove the saucepan from the heat and stir in the oats and optional ingredients.

7. Turn the mixture into the prepared tin. Smooth the top and press down well with the back of a metal spoon.

8. Bake for 20 mins. The flapjacks will be golden brown but will remain moist until they are fully cooled.

9. When baked, remove from the oven using oven gloves and cool in tin for 5 mins. Cut into wedges but cool completely before removing them from the tin.

10. Serve in wedges as they are or drizzle with the melted chocolate/crushed Crunchie bar.

TOP TIP

A properly lined tin makes your baked item easier to remove after cooking. To line the tin: Place the tin on top of the greaseproof paper, draw the shape of the tin and cut it out. Your paper will be the perfect size!

Evaluation

Date of Practical: _____

Q1. Personal Reflection: Did I ...?

Set up my unit correctly? ☐ ☐ ☐

Weigh and measure ingredients accurately? ☐ ☐ ☐

Preheat the oven to correct temperature? ☐ ☐ ☐

Melt the melting ingredients on a medium heat? ☐ ☐ ☐

Mix evenly and thoroughly? ☐ ☐ ☐

Flatten the mixture into the tin evenly? ☐ ☐ ☐

Bake until golden brown in colour? ☐ ☐ ☐

Slice into even-sized wedges? ☐ ☐ ☐

Cool completely in the tin? ☐ ☐ ☐

Keep a tidy and well-organised unit throughout? ☐ ☐ ☐

Prepare, serve and clean within the time available? ☐ ☐ ☐

Q2. Evaluate your dish using the following headings:

COLOUR _____

_____

FLAVOUR _____

_____

TEXTURE _____

_____

CRITICAL FRIEND _____

_____

_____

Q3. Based on your evaluation of the colour, flavour and texture and the comments of your critical friend, identify any changes you would make to your flapjacks.

_____

_____

_____

_____

Q4. Flapjacks are made using the melting method. Briefly explain how this method is carried out.

_____

_____

_____

_____

_____

_____

Q5. Optional activity: Sugar and syrup/honey are used in this basic recipe. This food is considered to be a high-sugar snack with a high GI level. Define the term 'high GI' and give a reason why this food is 'high GI'.

Definition:

_____

_____

Reason why this food is 'high GI':

_____

_____

Q6. Optional activity: Granola bars are a very popular snack item among teenagers. Homemade granola bars can be made with low-fat and low-sugar ingredients.

(a)   With your partner, research a recipe for a granola bar.

(b)   Compare the ingredients in the granola bar to those of your homemade flapjacks.

(c)   Write two additional statements to compare the nutritive value of these homemade snack items.

1.   Granola bars are made with less sugar than flapjacks. This makes them more suitable in a low-calorie diet.

2.   _____

3.   _____

23 Sponge with a Twist

Equipment

Chopping board(s) (colour-coded), sharp knife, weighing scales, mixing bowl, greaseproof paper, sieve, electric whisk, metal spoon, pastry brush, scissors, two sponge tins (cake)/one baking tray (Swiss roll), oven gloves, wire tray, cutlery, two large plates (for cutlery).

Method

1. HANDS, APRON, EQUIPMENT and SET UP UNIT.

2. Preheat the oven to 180°C/gas mark 4.

3. Weigh and measure all ingredients.

4. Grease and line sponge tins/baking tray with greaseproof paper.

5. Whisk eggs and sugar together until the mixture is thick, pale and creamy.

6. Sieve the flour high over the bowl and fold in gently with a metal spoon to prevent air loss – the more air, the lighter the sponge.

7. Divide the mixture evenly between the two sponge tins/pour into the baking tray.

8. Bake for 12–15 mins until spongy. To test for doneness, press with your finger – it should spring back with no indent left in the cake. It will also be shrinking back from the edges a little.

9. While the sponge mixture is baking, wash and chop the strawberries/wash raspberries.

10. Whip the fresh cream using an electric whisk/hand whisk. The cream should be roughly double in size and forming stiff peaks.

TOP TIP

Learn to check when egg and sugar mixtures are whisked adequately. Lift the beater out of the mixture. The mixture is thick enough if the mixture 'sits' on top and doesn't sink immediately.

Learning Intentions

★ Use a variety of preparation and cooking techniques to make this dish.

★ Demonstrate creative skills in serving this dish attractively.

★ Apply appropriate hygiene and safety rules when making this dish.

**Makes: 1 Swiss roll or an 8"
sponge**

50 mins

Perfect dish for all class lengths.

Ingredients

4 large eggs

100 g caster sugar

100 g self-raising flour

TO DECORATE:

227 ml cream (buy pre-whipped for 1-hr class)

5 strawberries/raspberries

2 tbsp strawberry/raspberry jam

icing sugar (to garnish)

Cake	Swiss roll
○ When the layers are cooked, use the oven gloves to remove from the oven and bring to the wire tray.	○ When the sponge is cooked, remove from the oven using oven gloves.
○ Leave them to cool and then turn both out from their tins and peel off the greaseproof paper attached to their undersides.	○ Place a piece of baking paper onto the wire tray and sprinkle with some caster sugar.
	○ Turn the sponge onto this sugared paper.
○ Add jam, cream and strawberries to one layer, and cover this layer with the other.	○ Remove greaseproof paper attached to the underside of the sponge.
	○ Roll the sponge up in the paper and leave it to cool.
○ Dredge with icing sugar to garnish.	○ Unroll the sponge and add the cream and raspberries before rolling it back up loosely to make a Swiss roll.
	○ Dredge with icing sugar to garnish.

Evaluation

Date of Practical: _____

Q1. Personal Reflection: Did I ...?

Set up my unit correctly? ☐ ☐ ☐

Weigh and measure ingredients accurately? ☐ ☐ ☐

Preheat the oven to correct temperature? ☐ ☐ ☐

Line the tin effectively to prevent sticking? ☐ ☐ ☐

Whisk eggs and sugar to the correct consistency? ☐ ☐ ☐

Fold flour gently to prevent loss of air? ☐ ☐ ☐

Cook in the tin appropriate for the cake being made? ☐ ☐ ☐

Check for doneness correctly? ☐ ☐ ☐

Whip cream to correct consistency? ☐ ☐ ☐

Decorate and serve the dish attractively? ☐ ☐ ☐

Keep a tidy and well-organised unit throughout? ☐ ☐ ☐

Prepare, serve and clean within the time available? ☐ ☐ ☐

Q2. Evaluate your dish using the following headings:

COLOUR _____

_____

FLAVOUR _____

_____

TEXTURE _____

_____

CRITICAL FRIEND _____

_____

Q3. Based on your evaluation of the colour, flavour and texture and the comments of your critical friend, identify any changes you would make to your sponge.

Q4. Identify where you applied specific hygiene and safety rules in the preparation and serving of this dish.

HYGIENE

SAFETY

Q5. Optional activity: This type of sponge cake is made using the whisking method. Briefly explain how this method is carried out.

Q6. Optional activity: Work with your partner to research how you could alter the flavours in this recipe. Make suggestions below and then try them at home.

Alternative flavours

24 Pastry

For one-hour classes: Pastry freezes very well. Make the pastry, then freeze. Thaw out before the next Home Economics class and make quiche, apple tart or sausage rolls, or if class is the next day, simply place the pastry in the fridge overnight.

Shortcrust Pastry

20 mins
for 200 g–220 g
shortcrust pastry

Shortcrust pastry is a pastry made from flour, fat (butter/ margarine) and a little cold water. It has a crumbly texture. It is used in the making of tarts, pies, sausage rolls, flans and quiches. See the shortcrust pastry ingredients list for each separate dish and use the method given here.

Equipment

Mixing bowl, sieve, butter knife, flour dredger, cling film, small jug, cutlery, two large plates (for cutlery).

Method

1. HANDS, APRON, EQUIPMENT and SET UP UNIT.
2. Weigh and measure all ingredients.
3. Sieve the flour and salt into the mixing bowl. Rub in the butter/ margarine with fingertips until it resembles breadcrumbs.
4. Add the cold water slowly and stir with a butter knife until it forms a soft dough.
5. Turn onto a floured board and knead lightly.
6. Wrap the pastry in cling film and put in the fridge.

Quiche

Serves: 6   **1 hr 10 mins**

Make pastry in advance to save time.

Equipment

Chopping board(s) (colour-coded), sharp knife, weighing scales, grater, measuring jug, fork, frying pan, 10" quiche dish, greaseproof paper, baking beans, mixing bowl, flour dredger, oven gloves, cutlery, two large plates (for cutlery).

Method

1. HANDS, APRON, EQUIPMENT and SET UP UNIT.
2. Preheat the oven to 200°C/gas mark 6.
3. Weigh and measure all ingredients.
4. Grease the quiche dish using a little butter/margarine.
5. Remove the pastry from the fridge and roll out on a floured table. Line the 10" quiche dish with the pastry and trim the edges while leaving a slight overlap. Line with greaseproof paper and fill with baking beans. Bake blind for 10–15 mins.
6. Peel and finely chop the onions. Chop the streaky bacon into cubes.

Ingredients

220 g shortcrust pastry (220 g plain flour, 110 g butter/margarine, 7–8 tbsp cold water, ½ tsp salt)

1 small red onion

1 small white onion

150 g chopped streaky bacon

½ tsp rosemary

½ tsp thyme

320 ml cream

3 medium eggs

salt and black pepper to taste

165 g strong Cheddar cheese

fresh parsley (to garnish)

7. Fry the bacon in a little olive oil until crisp, add the onions and fry until soft. Add the rosemary and thyme to the mix. Set aside in a bowl.

8. Remove the pastry from the oven using oven gloves, remove the greaseproof paper and baking beans, pierce the pastry base with a fork all over and return to the oven to cook for a further 5 mins, then remove with oven gloves.

9. Reduce the temperature of the oven to 180°C/gas mark 4.

10. Whisk the cream, eggs, salt and pepper.

11. Grate the cheese.

12. Sprinkle the bacon and onion mix on the pastry case, followed by the cheese, and pour the egg and cream mixture into the case.

13. Cook in the centre of the oven for 35–40 mins or until cooked and set, and slightly brown.

14. Remove from the oven using oven gloves and allow to cool for 5 mins before serving.

15. Garnish with fresh parsley.

TOP TIP

Pastry can be modified easily to keep it in line with Healthy Eating Guidelines, for example by using half-wholemeal and half-plain flour.

Apple Tart

Serves: 6   1 hr 10 mins

Make pastry in advance to save time.

Ingredients

220 g shortcrust pastry (220 g plain flour, 110 g butter/margarine, 7–8 tbsp cold water, ½ tsp salt)

3 cooking apples (5–6 stalks rhubarb can be used as an alternative to apples)

3 whole cloves/1 tsp cinnamon

sugar to sweeten

1 small egg, beaten (for glaze)

Equipment

Chopping board(s) (colour-coded), sharp knife, vegetable peeler, apple tart plate, flour dredger, pastry brush, fork, oven gloves, cutlery, two large plates (for cutlery).

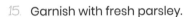

Method

1. HANDS, APRON, EQUIPMENT and SET UP UNIT.

2. Preheat the oven to 190°C/gas mark 5.

3. Weigh and measure all ingredients.

4. Grease the apple tart plate with a little butter.

5. Remove the pastry from the fridge and divide in two. Lightly flour the table and roll out each half of the pastry. When rolled out, each half should be slightly bigger than the plate. Place one half of the pastry on the greased plate.

6. Peel, core and slice apples thinly. Place the sliced apples on the pastry and sweeten each layer of apples with sugar. If using cloves or cinnamon, add at this point.

7. Using a pastry brush, brush the edge of the pastry with water. Place the second half of the pastry on top of the apple pie. Using a fork, press the outer edges together. Trim any excess pastry.

8. Using a pastry brush, glaze the top of the apple pie with beaten egg. Use a fork to prick the top of the apple pie – this allows steam to escape during the cooking process.

9. Bake for 10 mins at 190°C/gas mark 5 and then reduce heat to 180°C/gas mark 4 for 20–25 mins.

10. Remove from the oven using oven gloves and allow to cool slightly.

11. Serve with whipped cream, ice cream or custard.

Sausage Rolls

Serves: 8   1 hr

Make pastry in advance to save time.

Ingredients

200 g shortcrust pastry (200 g flour, 100 g butter/ margarine, 8–10 tbsp cold water, ½ tsp salt)

DELUXE SAUSAGE ROLLS

200 g shortcrust pastry

300 g sausage meat

1 clove garlic/1 tsp garlic granules

1 tsp thyme, rosemary, black pepper, basil and sage/5 tsp mixed herbs

50 g breadcrumbs

1 small egg

50 ml milk

QUICK AND EASY SAUSAGE ROLLS

200 g shortcrust pastry

300 g deskinned sausages

TO GLAZE

○ 1 small egg

○ 1 tbsp milk

fresh parsley (to garnish)

Equipment

Mixing bowl, garlic crusher, rolling pin, flour dredger, cup/jug, pastry brush, knife, serving plate, baking tray, oven gloves, cutlery, two large plates (for cutlery).

Method

1. HANDS, APRON, EQUIPMENT and SET UP UNIT.

2. Preheat the oven to 200°C/gas mark 6.

3. Weigh and measure all ingredients.

4. Peel and crush garlic.

5. For the deluxe sausage rolls, combine the sausage meat, herbs, garlic, breadcrumbs, milk and eggs in a bowl and mix together well.

6. Remove the pastry from the fridge and roll out on a floured work surface into a large rectangle, approximately the thickness of a €2 coin. Cut the pastry lengthways into two rectangles.

7. For the deluxe sausage rolls, on a lightly floured board, divide the sausage meat in two and roll both halves into a sausage shape the length of your pastry rectangle.

8. For the egg glaze, beat the egg and milk together in a cup or jug.

9. Lay the sausage meat on one half of the pastry, set back from the edge slightly, brush the edge with egg wash to seal and then wrap the other side of the pastry over the top and press down with your fingers or a fork.

10. For the quick and easy sausage rolls, lay the deskinned sausages on one half of the pastry and use the same method as described above.

11. Repeat the process again with the remaining pastry and sausage meat.

12. Cut the rolls to your desired size. Brush the tops with the remaining egg wash and cut two slits perpendicular across the top of the sausage rolls. Place on a lightly floured baking tray.

13. Bake for 10 mins, and then lower the heat to 180°C/gas mark 4 and cook for a further 10–15 mins until the pastry is golden and the sausage meat cooked through.

14. Remove from the oven using oven gloves, arrange attractively on a plate and serve hot, garnished with fresh parsley.

Evaluation

Date of Practical: _____

Q1. Personal Reflection: Did I ...?

Set up my unit correctly? ☐ ☐ ☐

Weigh and measure ingredients accurately? ☐ ☐ ☐

Preheat the oven to correct temperature? ☐ ☐ ☐

Rub the butter into the flour using fingertips only? ☐ ☐ ☐

Knead the dough lightly? ☐ ☐ ☐

Prepare the filling for the pastry dish correctly? ☐ ☐ ☐

Use the right cooking times? ☐ ☐ ☐

Wash hands after preparing raw meat? ☐ ☐ ☐

Check for doneness? ☐ ☐ ☐

Have a well-flavoured end product? ☐ ☐ ☐

Decorate and serve the dish attractively? ☐ ☐ ☐

Keep a tidy and well-organised unit throughout? ☐ ☐ ☐

Prepare, serve and clean within the time available? ☐ ☐ ☐

Q2. Evaluate your dish using the following headings:

COLOUR _____

_____

FLAVOUR _____

_____

TEXTURE _____

_____

CRITICAL FRIEND _____

_____

Q3. Based on your evaluation of the colour, flavour and texture and the comments of your critical friend, identify any changes you would make to your pastry dish.

_____

_____

_____

_____

Q4. When making quiche, the pastry is 'baked blind'. Explain this term.

_____

_____

_____

_____

_____

Q5. Optional activity: **Choosing one of the dishes (quiche/apple tart/sausage rolls), identify two modifications you could make to the ingredients list to help keep the dish in line with Healthy Eating Guidelines.**

Name of chosen dish:	
Healthy Eating Guideline	**Modification**
1.	
2.	

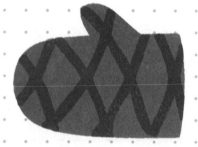

Q6. Optional activity: **Freezing prepared foods and dinners is an excellent way of reducing waste.**

(a) Research the purpose of freezing food.

(b) Give examples of four meals that can be made in advance and frozen.

(c) Identify four guidelines to follow when freezing food.

(d) List two important guidelines to follow when using frozen food.

UNIT 4
Desserts

25. CHOCOLATE BISCUIT CHRISTMAS PUDDING

26. MINI OREO CHEESECAKE

27. KEY LIME PIE

28. TRENDY BREAD AND BUTTER PUDDING

25 Chocolate Biscuit Christmas Pudding

TOP TIP

This mixture can also be used to make rocky road. Just spread it out flat in a baking tray, allow to set and then slice into bars to serve.

Serves: 6–8

30 mins
+ setting
+ decoration time

An overnight set (two nights max.) and decoration time (1 hr) is needed.

Ingredients

150 g butter

75 g caster sugar

160 g golden syrup

100 g drinking chocolate

325 g biscuit (mixture of rich tea, digestive and Maltesers)

OPTIONAL:
3 squares white chocolate/handful marshmallows/30 g hazelnuts/30 g raisins/ 1 Crunchie bar

TO DECORATE:
fondant icing (colour[s] of your choice) and icing sugar

TOP TIP

If using optional ingredients, use less biscuit to prevent dryness.

Equipment

Chopping board(s) (colour-coded), sharp knife, weighing scales, pudding bowl (or similar), cling film, mixing bowl, saucepan, metal spoon, wooden spoon, cake board, rolling pin, decorating tools such as cutters (if available), cutlery, two large plates (for cutlery).

Method

1. HANDS, APRON, EQUIPMENT and SET UP UNIT.

2. Weigh and measure all ingredients.

3. Line the pudding bowl with two layers of cling film. Press this well into the bowl.

4. Break the biscuits or chop them into uneven-sized pieces. Do this over the mixing bowl to catch all the crumbs. Add the Maltesers and other optional ingredients (except white chocolate, marshmallows or Crunchie bar, if using) to the mixing bowl.

5. Add the butter, sugar, syrup and drinking chocolate to a saucepan and melt over a medium heat, stirring constantly so that the mixture doesn't split or burn, until fully melted.

6. Pour the melted ingredients into the mixing bowl and fold gently so as not to break up the biscuit mixture any further.

7. If using white chocolate or a Crunchie bar, roughly chop and add at this point. Add marshmallows (if using) at this point.

8. Pour the combined mixture into the pudding bowl and push it down well with the back of a metal spoon.

9. Cover with cling film and set at room temperature overnight.

10. Once set, remove from bowl by tipping out the set mixture onto a cake board, and peel off the cling film.

11. Dredge icing sugar onto the table. Roll the fondant out with a rolling pin to a thickness of a €2 coin.

12. Cover the pudding completely with the fondant. Using the remaining fondant icing and decorating tools, decorate your chocolate Christmas pudding in a Christmas theme.

13. Serve as is. This pudding will keep in an airtight container for a week.

Evaluation

Date of Practical: _____

Q1. Personal Reflection: Did I ...?

Set up my unit correctly? ☐ ☐ ☐

Weigh and measure ingredients accurately? ☐ ☐ ☐

Melt without burning or splitting the mixture? ☐ ☐ ☐

Mix without further breaking the biscuit? ☐ ☐ ☐

Set the pudding fully? ☐ ☐ ☐

Roll the fondant to an even thickness? ☐ ☐ ☐

Have a well-flavoured end product? ☐ ☐ ☐

Decorate and serve the dish attractively? ☐ ☐ ☐

Keep a tidy and well-organised unit throughout? ☐ ☐ ☐

Prepare, serve and clean within the time available? ☐ ☐ ☐

Q2. Evaluate your dish using the following headings:

COLOUR _____

_____

FLAVOUR _____

_____

TEXTURE _____

_____

CRITICAL FRIEND _____

_____

Q3. Based on your evaluation of the colour, flavour and texture and the comments of your critical friend, identify any changes you would make to your pudding.

_____
_____
_____
_____
_____
_____
_____
_____

Q4. This recipe requires you to use fondant icing. List two rules to follow when using fondant icing.

Rule 1:

_____
_____
_____

Rule 2

_____
_____
_____

Q5. Optional activity: This pudding could be made with sugar-free or gluten-free biscuits and sweets to make it more suitable for those following special diets. Foods that have been designed for special diets are often quite expensive. Find out the cost of the following ingredients:

Packet regular digestive biscuits:	
Packet regular rich tea biscuits:	
Packet sugar-free biscuits (any variety):	
Packet gluten-free biscuits (any variety):	

Q6. Optional activity: Children receive many more Easter eggs today than what they did in the past.

(a) Ask an older relative if they received Easter eggs and how many they received. Record what they tell you.

(b) Research a recipe for rocky road slices which uses chocolate as an ingredient and try it out at Easter to use up any excess Easter eggs.

An older relative's experience of receiving Easter eggs	Rocky road recipe (using Easter egg chocolate)

26 Mini Oreo Cheesecake

TOP TIP

Alter the recipe: double the ingredients and make it in a cheesecake tin, or make small cheesecakes in cupcake cases. Add mint essence to the filling and use mint-flavoured Oreo cookies. The options are limitless!

Serves: 2

40 mins
+ extra for refrigeration

Perfect dish for all class lengths.

Ingredients

BASE:
10 Oreo cookies

30 g butter

FILLING:
4 Oreo cookies

200 g cream cheese/ mascarpone

100 ml double cream

30 g caster sugar

1 tsp vanilla essence

TOPPING:
remainder of carton of cream/grated chocolate/ a portion of the base held back to sprinkle on top

TOP TIP

This is a great opportunity to try out your piping skills. Your teacher will show you how to assemble a piping bag. Practise your piping skills on a plate first before moving on to your dessert.

Equipment

Chopping board(s) (colour-coded), sharp knife, weighing scales, measuring jug, rolling pin, sealed food bag, saucepan, mixing bowl, wooden spoon, electric whisk, two serving glasses, piping bag, cutlery, two large plates (for cutlery).

Method

1. HANDS, APRON, EQUIPMENT and SET UP UNIT.

2. Weigh and measure all ingredients.

3. *To make the base:* Place the Oreos on the chopping board and use the rolling pin to crush them into crumbs/place in a partly sealed food bag and crush using rolling pin. (Do not fully seal the bag as this can cause it to burst. The bag can be washed out afterwards and reused, to avoid waste.) Melt the butter over a gentle heat in the saucepan, taking care not to burn it. Remove from the heat and mix in the crushed Oreos. Stir well and leave aside.

4. *To make the filling:* Chop the Oreos into small pieces or crush as before. Add cream cheese, cream, sugar and vanilla essence into a mixing bowl and whisk on a high speed until combined and thickened slightly. Stir through the Oreos mixture.

5. Take the serving glasses to the table. Place a small amount of the base in the bottom of the glass and push it down with the back of a spoon. Carefully spoon a generous amount of the filling on top. Repeat the process, adding another layer of cookies and filling until it is all used.

6. Whip the remaining cream until it has doubled in size and is forming stiff peaks. Spoon or pipe onto the top of the mixtures in the glasses. Sprinkle reserved base or grated chocolate over the cream.

7. Place the cheesecakes in the fridge to set. This takes about two hours and could be done at home or the cake could be collected at the end of the school day.

8. Serve it as is after setting.

Evaluation

Date of Practical: _____

Q1. Personal Reflection: Did I ...?

Set up my unit correctly? ☐ ☐ ☐

Weigh and measure ingredients accurately? ☐ ☐ ☐

Crush biscuit into crumbs? ☐ ☐ ☐

Melt butter without burning it? ☐ ☐ ☐

Make a thick, creamy filling? ☐ ☐ ☐

Layer the cheesecakes into the glasses neatly? ☐ ☐ ☐

Whip cream to correct consistency? ☐ ☐ ☐

Show piping skills? ☐ ☐ ☐

Have a well-flavoured end product? ☐ ☐ ☐

Decorate and serve the dish attractively? ☐ ☐ ☐

Keep a tidy and well-organised unit throughout? ☐ ☐ ☐

Prepare, serve and clean within the time available? ☐ ☐ ☐

Q2. Evaluate your dish using the following headings:

COLOUR _____

_____

FLAVOUR _____

_____

TEXTURE _____

_____

CRITICAL FRIEND _____

_____

Q3. Based on your evaluation of the colour, flavour and texture and the comments of your critical friend, identify any changes you would make to your cheesecake.

_____

_____

_____

_____

_____

_____

_____

Q4. Identify a new skill you learned while making this dish. Evaluate how effectively you carried out this skill.

New skill: _____

_____

Effectiveness of implementation: _____

_____

_____

Q5. Optional activity: Double cream has been used in this recipe. Its higher fat content means it obtains a thick consistency when whisked, which is desirable for making a cheesecake. Investigate the fat content of the following types of cream:

Cream	Fat content per 100 ml
Double cream	
Single cream	
Sour cream	
Low-fat cream	

Q6. Optional activity: As a class, have a competition to see who can make the most effective piping bag. Go online to find out how to make a piping bag. Half the class will make a piping bag using greaseproof paper while the other half will use a strong sandwich bag. Use them to decorate your cheesecake and evaluate them under the following headings:

Compare	Greaseproof paper	Sandwich bag
Effectiveness		
Sustainability		

27 Key Lime Pie

Learning Intentions

☆ Demonstrate the correct culinary techniques required to prepare and serve this dish.

☆ Apply appropriate hygiene and safety rules when making this dish.

☆ Evaluate the sensory attributes of this dish and its contribution to a healthy diet.

☆ Demonstrate creative skills in serving this dish attractively.

Serves: 8

30 mins prep
+ 2 hrs setting/overnight

In a one-hour class, bring in your own flan dish or cheese cake tin and collect from the Home Economics kitchen before going home.

Ingredients

300 g ginger nut biscuits (digestive biscuits can also be used)

150 g butter

250 ml double cream

400 g can condensed milk

6–8 limes, depending on preference

FOR DECORATION (OPTIONAL):

1 tbsp icing sugar

100 ml cream

zest of 1 lime

Equipment

Food processor/sealed food bag and rolling pin, small saucepan, large bowl, 10" flan tin/dish or eight ramekin dishes, metal spoon, grater, juicer, large mixing bowl, electric mixer, spatula, piping bag, cutlery, two large plates (for cutlery).

TOP TIP

This is a relatively easy dessert to make and ideal for a special occasion. The quantities given would make eight individual portions in ramekin dishes. This is an extra special way of serving this dish and is also a helpful way of ensuring that portion sizes are not too large.

Method

1. HANDS, APRON, EQUIPMENT and SET UP UNIT.

2. Weigh and measure all ingredients.

3. Place the ginger nut biscuits into a food processor and blitz/place in a partly sealed food bag and crush using rolling pin. (Do not fully seal the bag as this can cause it to burst. The bag can be washed out afterwards and reused, to avoid waste.)

4. In a microwave or small saucepan, melt the butter and pour into the food processor with the biscuit crumb. Blitz again/stir the melted butter into the crushed biscuit in a large bowl.

5. Spoon the biscuit mixture into a flan dish and press into the base and sides evenly.

6. Wash the limes, then roll each for 30 secs on a chopping board (this helps to release the juice). Zest all but one of the limes using the fine side of the grater, only removing the green skin and being careful not to grate down to the pith. Halve each lime and juice using the juicer.

7. In a large mixing bowl, beat the double cream, condensed milk, lime juice and lime zest with an electric mixer until the mixture is thick.

8. Pour the filling mixture on top of the biscuit base. Place in the fridge and chill for a few hours or ideally overnight.

9. To serve, whip the cream and icing sugar together and pipe on top of the key lime pie. Grate the zest of the remaining lime on top.

Evaluation

Date of Practical: _____

Q1. Personal Reflection: Did I ...?

Set up my unit correctly? ☐ ☐ ☐

Weigh and measure ingredients accurately? ☐ ☐ ☐

Crush the biscuits using a food processor/a partly sealed food bag and rolling pin? ☐ ☐ ☐

Press the biscuit mixture evenly into the base and sides of the flan dish? ☐ ☐ ☐

Grate only the zest from the limes? ☐ ☐ ☐

Extract maximum juice when juicing the limes? ☐ ☐ ☐

Whip the cream, condensed milk, lime juice and lime zest until thick? ☐ ☐ ☐

Pour the whipped mixture into the biscuit base and leave to set? ☐ ☐ ☐

Decorate and serve the dish attractively? ☐ ☐ ☐

Have a well-flavoured end product? ☐ ☐ ☐

Keep a tidy and well-organised unit throughout? ☐ ☐ ☐

Prepare, serve and clean within the time available? ☐ ☐ ☐

Q2. Evaluate your dish using the following headings:

COLOUR _____
_____

FLAVOUR _____
_____

TEXTURE _____
_____

CRITICAL FRIEND _____
_____

Q3. Based on your evaluation of the colour, flavour and texture and the comments of your critical friend, identify any changes you would make to your key lime pie.

_____
_____
_____
_____
_____
_____

Q4. Identify where you applied specific hygiene and safety rules in the preparation and serving of this dish.

HYGIENE _____
_____

SAFETY _____
_____

Q5. Optional activity: Key lime pie is a suitable dessert for a special occasion. Give two nutritive reasons why it is important not to include desserts such as key lime pie as part of our everyday menu.

Reason 1:
_____
_____

Reason 2:
_____
_____

Q6. Optional activity: In this recipe it is suggested that the butter can be melted in a microwave. Answer these questions in relation to microwave-cooking:

(a) State two advantages and two disadvantages of cooking food in a microwave.

(b) Identify two types of cookware not suitable for using in a microwave.

(c) Identify two types of cookware suitable for using in a microwave.

(d) State four different uses of a microwave.

28 Trendy Bread and Butter Pudding

TOP TIP

Fresh or dried blueberries can be used as an alternative to sultanas/raisins. Grated chocolate or chocolate chips can be added to bread and butter pudding for an even sweeter twist!

Serves: 6   50 mins–1 hr

In a one-hour class, bring in your own flan dish, ovenproof dish or cheese cake tin and collect from the Home Economics kitchen before going home.

Ingredients

50 g butter, and extra for greasing

8 slices white sliced loaf (brioche, hot cross buns and croissants are also suitable)

100 g sultanas/raisins/ mixture of both

grated rind of 1 lemon/ 1 orange

1½ tsp cinnamon

1½ tsp nutmeg

3 whole eggs, plus 1 egg yolk

70 g caster sugar

250 ml milk

300 ml cream

1 tsp vanilla extract

1 tbsp sugar to sprinkle

Equipment

Chopping board(s) (colour-coded), sharp knife, weighing scales, rectangular ovenproof dish, butter knife, grater, mixing bowl, whisk, saucepan, oven gloves, cutlery, two large plates (for cutlery).

Method

1. HANDS, APRON, EQUIPMENT and SET UP UNIT.

2. Preheat the oven to 180°C/gas mark 4.

3. Weigh and measure all ingredients.

4. Grease your dish with a little butter.

5. Butter the bread and cut each slice into four triangles.

6. Zest the lemon and mix it with the cinnamon, nutmeg and dried fruit.

7. Place a layer of the bread slices in the bottom of the dish, butter-side down. Sprinkle half the dried fruit and spice mixture over this layer.

8. Use the remaining bread for the second layer and the remaining dried fruit and spice mixture with this layer.

9. Beat the eggs and sugar together with a whisk.

10. Pour the milk and cream into a saucepan and heat until steaming, but do not boil.

11. Pour the milk and cream mixture over the eggs and sugar, whisk gently until smooth and add the vanilla extract.

TOP TIP

It is important that you do not allow the milk and cream to boil, as you might burn it and cause a film to form on top. As well as that, you might have a hob to clean up if the milk and cream boils and bubbles over!

12. Pour this mixture over the bread. Sprinkle a tablespoon of sugar over the top.

13. Place in the oven for 30–35 mins until set and turning brown on top.

14. Remove from the oven using oven gloves and serve hot, accompanied with a scoop of ice cream or freshly whipped cream.

Evaluation

Date of Practical: _____

Q1. Personal Reflection: Did I ...?

Set up my unit correctly? ☐ ☐ ☐

Preheat the oven to correct temperature? ☐ ☐ ☐

Weigh and measure ingredients accurately? ☐ ☐ ☐

Prepare the bread correctly? ☐ ☐ ☐

Heat the milk and cream to the correct temperature? ☐ ☐ ☐

Pour the milk and cream over the eggs and sugar and stir? ☐ ☐ ☐

Assemble the dish in the correct order? ☐ ☐ ☐

Bake for the correct length of time? ☐ ☐ ☐

Have a well-flavoured end product? ☐ ☐ ☐

Keep a tidy and well-organised unit throughout? ☐ ☐ ☐

Prepare, serve and clean within the time available? ☐ ☐ ☐

Q2. Evaluate your dish using the following headings:

COLOUR _____

_____

FLAVOUR _____

_____

TEXTURE _____

_____

CRITICAL FRIEND _____

_____

Q3. Based on your evaluation of the colour, flavour and texture and the comments of your critical friend, identify any changes you would make to your bread and butter pudding.

_____

_____

_____

_____

Q4. The ovenproof dish used for baking the bread and butter pudding was greased. State an advantage of doing this.

_____

_____

_____

Q5. Optional activity: Plan a three-course main meal with bread and butter pudding as the dessert. Ensure this menu is balanced (three food groups).

MENU

Starter

Main Course and Drink

Dessert

Balanced Food Check

Fruit/Veg
☐

Breads/Cereals
☐

Dairy
☐

Meat/Alternatives
☐

Q6. Optional activity: Leftover bread/bread that will go stale can be used in bread and butter pudding. This is a great example of food sustainability. In pairs, discuss the following questions:

(a) What is food sustainability?

(b) Are there any foods that regularly go to waste in your home?

(c) What do you think are the main reasons for these foods going to waste in your home?

(d) Can you identify three ways of helping to prevent the food waste you have identified in your home?

UNIT 5
Meat

29. CHICKEN NUGGETS AND SPICY POTATO WEDGES

30. STIR-FRY FOR EVERY OCCASION

31. FAJITAS

32. CHICKEN TIKKA MASALA

33. DELICIOUSLY CREAMY PAPRIKA CHICKEN

34. SPAGHETTI BOLOGNESE

35. CHILLI TWO-WAYS

36. MEATBALLS IN SPICY TOMATO SAUCE

37. STEAK SANDWICH

29 Chicken Nuggets and Spicy Potato Wedges

Serves: 3–4   **50 mins**

In a one-hour class, leave out the wedges or the dipping sauce to save on time.

Ingredients

FOR THE NUGGETS:

75 g plain flour

2 eggs

100 g breadcrumbs

50 g parmesan cheese

cupful cornflakes

salt and pepper

2 chicken breast fillets (alternatively use fish or prawns)

FOR THE DIPPING SAUCE:

50 g mayonnaise

2 tbsp sweet chilli sauce/ 1 clove garlic

FOR THE WEDGES:

1 bag baby potatoes

2 tbsp oil

2 tsp chilli powder/spices of your choice

Learning Intentions

★ Use a variety of preparation and cooking techniques to make this dish.

★ Apply appropriate hygiene and safety rules when making this dish.

★ Evaluate the sensory attributes of this dish and its contribution to a healthy diet.

★ Interpret information on a food label to compare my ingredients with those used in commercial chicken nuggets.

Equipment

Chopping board(s) (colour-coded), sharp knife, grater, sealable food bag, rolling pin, meat scissors, mixing bowl, two baking trays, garlic crusher, serving plate, serving bowl, cutlery, two large plates (for cutlery).

Method

1. HANDS, APRON, EQUIPMENT and SET UP UNIT.

2. Preheat the oven to 180°C/gas mark 4.

3. Weigh and measure all ingredients.

4. (If making wedges) Wash the potatoes, cut into quarters and place in a mixing bowl. Add the oil and spices and stir to coat thoroughly.

5. Place the potatoes on a tray and bake for 20–25 mins until they are browned and crispy.

6. Put the flour on a plate.

7. Whisk the two eggs in a bowl.

8. Grate the cheese using the fine side of the grater.

9. Put the cornflakes in a partly sealed food bag and roll them into crumbs using a rolling pin. (Do not fully seal the bag as this can cause it to burst. The bag can be washed out afterwards and reused, to avoid waste.)

10. Mix the breadcrumbs, cheese, cornflakes and salt and pepper in a mixing bowl.

11. Cut up the chicken into bite-sized chunks/ strips using the meat scissors.

12. Dip the chicken into the flour, then dip it into the egg and finally the breadcrumb mixture.

13. Place the nuggets on the baking tray, drizzle with a little oil and bake for 10–15 mins until the chicken is cooked through.

14. To make the dipping sauce, mix the mayonnaise and the sweet chilli sauce/crushed garlic and decant into a serving bowl.

15. Serve the nuggets and wedges with the dipping sauce on a large sharing plate.

> **TOP TIP**
>
> Sweet potato adds extra colour and would be an interesting alternative to baby potato. Chop them in half lengthways and then into wedges.

Evaluation

Date of Practical: _____

Q1. Personal Reflection: Did I ...?

Set up my unit correctly? ☐ ☐ ☐

Preheat the oven to correct temperature? ☐ ☐ ☐

Chop wedges into even-sized pieces? ☐ ☐ ☐

Coat wedges in oil evenly? ☐ ☐ ☐

Cut chicken into even-sized pieces? ☐ ☐ ☐

Use flour–egg–breadcrumbs system to fully coat the chicken pieces? ☐ ☐ ☐

Wash hands after preparing raw meat? ☐ ☐ ☐

Achieve crisp wedges and chicken? ☐ ☐ ☐

Make a tasty dipping sauce? ☐ ☐ ☐

Serve the dish attractively? ☐ ☐ ☐

Keep a tidy and well-organised unit throughout? ☐ ☐ ☐

Prepare, serve and clean within the time available? ☐ ☐ ☐

Q2. Evaluate your dish using the following headings:

COLOUR _____

_____

FLAVOUR _____

_____

TEXTURE _____

_____

CRITICAL FRIEND _____

_____

Q3. Based on your evaluation of the colour, flavour and texture and the comments of your critical friend, identify any changes you would make to your chicken nuggets and spicy potato wedges.

_____

_____

_____

_____

_____

_____

_____

_____

Q4. The chicken is coated using flour first, then egg and then breadcrumbs. State the reason for using each in this specific order.

_____

_____

_____

_____

_____

Q5. Optional activity: State a nutritional advantage of using the following fish in this recipe instead of chicken:

Salmon: _____

_____

Cod: _____

_____

Q6. Optional activity: Chicken nuggets are a popular convenience food for children and teenagers. Purchase a packet of commercial chicken nuggets and use the label or research online to identify the ingredients used in their manufacture. Divide the ingredients into food ingredients and additives.

Food ingredients	Additives

Are you surprised with your findings?   Yes ☐ No ☐

Based on the time it took to make the homemade nuggets and the information you gathered on the ingredients in commercial chicken nuggets, state how likely you are to make these homemade nuggets again:

Very likely ☐
Likely ☐
Not likely ☐

Give two reasons for your answer:

1.
2.

30 Stir-Fry for Every Occasion

Serves: 3–4   **40 mins**

Perfect dish for all class lengths.

Ingredients

Many foods are suitable for stir-frying. With your cooking partner, choose one protein food, 2–5 vegetables (depending on class length), aromatics, sauce ingredients and garnishes to complete your recipe. You'll get great ideas for flavour combinations online, or be adventurous and try your own!

PROTEIN
chicken, pork, beef, lamb, prawns, tofu, nuts, seeds

VEGETABLE
onion, peppers, mushrooms, carrot, baby corn, mange tout, broccoli, courgette, pak choi, bean sprouts, *any other vegetable of your choosing*

AROMATIC
garlic, ginger, fresh chilli, herbs, spices

SAUCE
soya sauce, sesame oil, chilli sauce, hoisin sauce, white rice vinegar, chicken stock, coconut milk, oyster sauce, honey, lemon/lime juice, fish sauce

GARNISH
scallions, seeds, nuts, fresh herbs, fresh chilli

POSSIBLE ACCOMPANIMENT:
rice/noodles

Equipment

Chopping board(s) (colour-coded), sharp knife, peeler, grater, garlic crusher, meat scissors, wooden spoon, wok, measuring jug, colander, cutlery, two large plates (for cutlery).

Method

1. HANDS, APRON, EQUIPMENT and SET UP UNIT.

2. Cut the meat into even-sized strips using the meat scissors.

3. Wash and prepare vegetables as necessary: top and tail, peel and slice the onion, halve, deseed and slice the peppers, destalk and slice/quarter the mushrooms, top and tail, peel and cut the carrots into batons/thin circles.

4. Prepare the aromatic ingredients and mix the sauce ingredients in a measuring jug.

5. Take all ingredients to the hob area.

6. If using rice, put it on to cook at this stage. (Rinse it first in cold water if it is very starchy.) To cook the rice: cover it generously with boiling water and boil for 12 mins. Rice should be swollen and fluffy. Strain in a colander when cooked.

7. Heat a tablespoon of vegetable oil in the wok.

8. Add ingredients to the wok in the following order:

   ○ Uncooked protein until it is almost cooked (3–5 mins). Prawns and tofu should be removed to a plate at this stage and added in at the end with the sauce ingredients. Other proteins remain in the wok at this point.

   ○ Aromatic ingredients for 1 min or less.

   ○ Hard vegetables, e.g. onion, baby corn, carrot for 3 mins.

   ○ Softer vegetables, e.g. peppers, courgette for 3 mins.

   ○ Sauce ingredients until heated through (approx. 2 mins).

9. Stir the ingredients to ensure even cooking and prevent scorching. The vegetables should be cooked al dente and the meat should be moist.

10. Remove from the wok to the serving dish and use your chosen garnish to decorate.

11. Serve with a suitable accompaniment such as rice or noodles.

> **TOP TIP**
> This recipe is easily adapted to become a chow mein. Use garlic, ginger, Chinese five spice and soya sauce as the aromatic and sauce ingredients. Add noodles to complete the dish.

Evaluation

Date of Practical: _____

Q1. Personal Reflection: Did I ...?

Set up my unit correctly?	☐ ☐ ☐	
Slice my meat evenly?	☐ ☐ ☐	
Wash hands after preparing raw meat?	☐ ☐ ☐	
Slice vegetables into even slices?	☐ ☐ ☐	
Heat oil until hot?	☐ ☐ ☐	
Add ingredients in the correct order?	☐ ☐ ☐	
Stir my ingredients constantly?	☐ ☐ ☐	

Use the right cooking times for each ingredient?   ☐ ☐ ☐

Have vegetables that were al dente?   ☐ ☐ ☐

Have meat that was moist?   ☐ ☐ ☐

Have a well-flavoured end product?   ☐ ☐ ☐

Serve the dish attractively?   ☐ ☐ ☐

Keep a tidy and well-organised unit throughout?   ☐ ☐ ☐

Prepare, serve and clean within the time available?   ☐ ☐ ☐

Q2. Evaluate your dish using the following headings:

COLOUR _____
_____

FLAVOUR _____
_____

TEXTURE _____
_____

CRITICAL FRIEND _____
_____

Q3. Based on your evaluation of the colour, flavour and texture and the comments of your critical friend, identify any changes you would make to your stir-fry.

_____

_____

_____

_____

_____

_____

_____

Q4. Identify where you applied specific hygiene and safety rules in the preparation and serving of this dish.

HYGIENE _____

_____

SAFETY _____

_____

Q5. Optional activity: Using the ingredients list provided above, identify two sets of ingredients that could be used to adapt this stir-fry to two specific diets of your choice.

Diet	Modifications

Q6. Optional activity: In small groups, research one of the following topics. Prepare a short summary of your research for the rest of the class.

List the effects of stir-frying on the nutritive value of foods.	Name the safety rules to follow when using a wok.	Research 'smoke point' and 'flash point' in relation to the use of oil during cooking.
Research how palm oil has affected the environment.	List five foods that are unsuitable for stir-frying. Give a reason why they are unsuitable.	Research the cooking oils that can withstand high heat most effectively.
Research the possibility of stir-frying without oil.	Research the different types of woks used for stir-frying.	Research the first-aid treatment for a minor burn.

31 Fajitas

Learning Intentions

☆ Use a variety of preparation and cooking techniques to make this dish.

☆ Apply appropriate hygiene and safety rules when making this dish.

☆ Demonstrate creative skills in choosing accompaniments to serve this dish attractively.

☆ Evaluate the sensory attributes of this dish and its contribution to a healthy diet.

Serves: 2–3　　**45 mins**

Perfect dish for all class lengths.

Ingredients

FOR THE MARINADE:

2 cloves garlic

juice of 1 lime

1 tsp chilli powder

1 tsp ground cumin

2 tsp smoked paprika

1 tsp ground coriander

handful fresh coriander

1 tbsp olive oil

2 chicken fillets/250 g stir-fry beef/12 prawns

1 red pepper ⎫
1 green pepper ⎬ just one pepper in a 1-hr class
1 yellow pepper ⎭

1 red onion

OPTIONAL VEGETABLES:

baby corn, mange tout, mushrooms

1 packet tortilla bread (preferably wholemeal)

OPTIONAL ACCOMPANIMENTS:

lettuce, salsa, sour cream, guacamole, grated cheese

Equipment

Chopping board(s) (colour-coded), sharp knife, garlic crusher, meat scissors, juicer, mixing bowl, wok/frying pan, wooden spoon, tin foil, two large plates, lazy Susan or similar serving plate, cutlery, two large plates (for cutlery).

Method

1. HANDS, APRON, EQUIPMENT and SET UP UNIT.

2. Weigh and measure all ingredients.

3. Peel and crush the garlic. Halve and juice the lime.

4. Mix all the marinade ingredients together in a mixing bowl.

5. Cut the chicken/beef into small, even strips using the meat scissors.

6. Add the chicken/beef/prawns to the marinade and mix well to coat.

7. Cover with cling film and put in the fridge.

8. Wash, halve, deseed and chop the peppers into even slices.

9. Top and tail, peel and finely slice the onion.

10. *Optional ingredients:* Slice the baby corn in half lengthways, wash the mange tout, wash and quarter the mushrooms.

11. Heat oil in the wok/frying pan. Add the chicken/beef and stir-fry until it has completely changed colour. If using prawns, stir-fry for 1–2 mins only.

12. Add the onions (baby corn/mange tout) and stir-fry for another 2 mins.

13. Add the pepper (mushrooms) and stir-fry for another 2 mins.

14. Heat the tortillas in the microwave for 1 min and wrap in tin foil to keep warm.

15. Serve fajitas with all accompaniments on a lazy Susan or just in the middle of the table. This is an ideal opportunity to make the salsa and guacamole you learned how to make in Recipe 12.

> **TOP TIP**
>
> The meat is marinated to add flavour. In class, marinade for as long as possible, but at home the meat can be left in the marinade overnight to further enhance the flavours.

Evaluation

Date of Practical: _____

Q1. Personal Reflection: Did I ...?

Set up my unit correctly? ☐ ☐ ☐

Use my knife safely? ☐ ☐ ☐

Measure marinade ingredients accurately? ☐ ☐ ☐

Slice meat thinly and evenly? ☐ ☐ ☐

Marinade meat for as long as possible? ☐ ☐ ☐

Wash hands after preparing raw meat? ☐ ☐ ☐

Slice vegetables thinly and evenly? ☐ ☐ ☐

Heat oil before cooking the meat? ☐ ☐ ☐

Add ingredients in the correct order? ☐ ☐ ☐

Have a well-flavoured end product? ☐ ☐ ☐

Serve the dish attractively? ☐ ☐ ☐

Keep a tidy and well-organised unit throughout? ☐ ☐ ☐

Prepare, serve and clean within the time available? ☐ ☐ ☐

Q2. Evaluate your dish using the following headings:

COLOUR _____

_____

FLAVOUR _____

_____

TEXTURE _____

_____

CRITICAL FRIEND _____

_____

Q3. Based on your evaluation of the colour, flavour and texture and the comments of your critical friend, identify any changes you would make to your fajitas.

_____

_____

_____

_____

_____

_____

Q5. Optional activity: Shellfish is a popular ingredient in modern cuisine and is increasingly more available. Compare shellfish and red meat under the following headings:

Compare	Shellfish	Red meat
Protein content		
Fat content		
Cost per 100 g (use the costing template on p. 187)		
Availability		

Q4. State one advantage and one disadvantage of stir-frying as a method of cooking.

Advantage: _____

_____

_____

_____

Disadvantage: _____

_____

_____

_____

Q6. Optional activity: In small groups, investigate different ways of assembling your fajita. Write/draw your favourite method below.

32 Chicken Tikka Masala

Serves 3–4   **50 mins**

In a one-hour class, reduce the quantity of rice to 150 g or omit.

Ingredients

3 chicken breasts

1 onion

1 red pepper

1 green pepper

1 tsp fresh ginger

2 cloves garlic

100 g natural yogurt

1 tbsp tomato purée

2 tbsp mango chutney

1 tsp sugar

4 tbsp Tikka Masala paste

1 tbsp olive oil

½ tin chopped tomatoes

300 g rice

fresh coriander (to garnish)

Equipment

Chopping board(s) (colour-coded), sharp knife, meat scissors, peeler, grater, garlic crusher, tin opener, wok/large saucepan, wooden spoon, measuring jug, cutlery, two large plates (for cutlery).

Method

1. HANDS, APRON, EQUIPMENT and SET UP UNIT.

2. Weigh and measure all ingredients.

3. Cut the chicken into bite-size pieces using the meat scissors.

4. Prepare vegetables: top and tail, peel and dice the onion, wash, halve, deseed and slice the peppers.

5. Peel and finely grate a small piece of ginger.

6. Peel and crush the garlic.

7. In a bowl, mix together the yogurt, ginger, garlic, tomato purée, mango chutney, sugar and Tikka Masala paste. Add the chicken, stir and coat well.

8. Heat the oil in a large saucepan or wok and sauté the onion until soft.

9. Once the onion is cooked, add the chicken mixture and cook for 5 mins.

10. Add the peppers and chopped tomatoes and allow the curry to simmer gently for 20 mins. The meat should be moist and the vegetables al dente.

11. Put the rice on to cook. (See Recipe 30 for details on how to prepare and cook rice.)

12. Serve the curry on a bed of rice. Garnish with coriander.

TOP TIP

A curry paste is a prepared blend of spices. Instead of using a shop-bought paste, experiment with making your own as this will result in a more authentic taste. If time allows, leave the chicken marinating for a few hours as this helps to tenderise the chicken and to develop a greater depth of flavour.

TOP TIP

Lamb can also be used in this dish, however it requires a longer cooking time. Ask your butcher for advice on how long a particular cut of lamb will take to cook.

Evaluation

Date of Practical: _____

Q1. Personal Reflection: Did I ...?

Set up my unit correctly?	☐ ☐ ☐	
Slice the chicken evenly?	☐ ☐ ☐	
Wash hands after preparing raw meat?	☐ ☐ ☐	
Slice vegetables into even slices?	☐ ☐ ☐	
Heat oil until hot?	☐ ☐ ☐	
Add ingredients in the correct order?	☐ ☐ ☐	
Use the right cooking times for each ingredient?	☐ ☐ ☐	

Have moist meat?	☐ ☐ ☐	
Have vegetables that were al dente?	☐ ☐ ☐	
Cook the rice in the correct way?	☐ ☐ ☐	
Have a well-flavoured end product?	☐ ☐ ☐	
Serve the dish attractively?	☐ ☐ ☐	
Keep a tidy and well-organised unit throughout?	☐ ☐ ☐	
Prepare, serve and clean within the time available?	☐ ☐ ☐	

Q2. Evaluate your dish using the following headings:

COLOUR _____

_____

FLAVOUR _____

_____

TEXTURE _____

_____

CRITICAL FRIEND _____

_____

Q3. Based on your evaluation of the colour, flavour and texture and the comments of your critical friend, identify any changes you would make to your chicken Tikka Masala.

_____

_____

_____

_____

Q4. Rice is a suitable accompaniment for this dish. State two guidelines to follow for cooking rice.

Guideline 1: _____

_____

Guideline 2: _____

_____

Q5. Optional activity: Chicken is a nutritious food. Evaluate the nutritional and dietetic contribution of chicken to our diet. Include four points of information.

Nutrient	Value to the diet

Q6. Optional activity: Working in pairs, choose one of the curries from the box. Briefly research the following:

(a) The country with which the curry is associated.

(b) The distinct flavour of the curry.

(c) The spices used in the curry.

(d) The level of hotness of the curry.

Tarkari	Jalfrezi	Green curry
Vindaloo	Rendang	Massaman

33 Deliciously Creamy Paprika Chicken

☆ Demonstrate the correct culinary techniques required to prepare and cook this dish.

☆ Apply appropriate hygiene and safety rules when making this dish.

☆ Evaluate the sensory attributes of this dish and its contribution to a healthy diet.

Serves: 2–3   **45 mins**

Perfect dish for all class lengths.

Equipment

Chopping board(s) (colour-coded), sharp knife, weighing scales, saucepan, measuring jug, garlic crusher, heavy-based pan/wok, wooden spoon, colander, serving dish, cutlery, two large plates (for cutlery).

Method

1. HANDS, APRON, EQUIPMENT and SET UP UNIT.

2. Weigh and measure all ingredients.

3. Place the pasta in a saucepan of boiling water, add a pinch of salt and a teaspoon of olive oil. Bring back to the boil and allow to simmer for 8–10 mins until the pasta is cooked al dente.

4. Using the measuring jug, add 200 ml of boiling water to a stock cube and stir until the stock cube has dissolved. Alternatively, use homemade chicken stock.

5. Cut the chicken into bite-sized pieces using the meat scissors.

6. Finely dice the chorizo.

7. Wash, deseed and slice the pepper. Peel and slice the onions. Peel and crush the garlic. Wash and slice the mushrooms.

8. Heat the vegetable oil in a large, heavy-based pan (ideally) or wok. Cook the chicken on a medium to high heat for 3–4 mins until the meat has turned white all over.

9. Add the chorizo, onions, garlic and mushrooms, then turn down the heat to a low to medium setting. Cover with a lid and sweat the ingredients for 3 mins. Add the peppers and sauté for a further 3 mins.

10. Add the flour and paprika to the mixture in the pan and stir until combined, taking care not to burn it.

11. Add the stock in small amounts and stir after each addition. If the mixture appears dry, add a little more stock. Simmer for 10 mins with the lid on.

12. Strain the pasta using the colander. ⚠

13. When the chicken is cooked, remove from the heat, add the pasta, stir in the cream and simmer for 1 min while stirring. The chicken should be moist and the vegetables al dente.

14. Serve hot, add black pepper and salt to taste and garnish with fresh parsley.

Ingredients

150 g penne pasta

pinch salt

1 tbsp olive oil

200 ml chicken stock

2 diced chicken fillets

100 g chorizo

1 red pepper

1 small red onion

1 small white onion

2 cloves garlic

4 medium closed-cup mushrooms

1 tbsp vegetable oil

1 tbsp plain flour

2 tsp smoked paprika

150/200 ml single cream

black pepper and salt to taste

fresh parsley (to garnish)

TOP TIP

When making this dish, sour cream can be used instead of regular cream. Sour cream gives a deeper taste, whereas regular cream gives a creamier taste.

Evaluation

Date of Practical: _____

Q1. Personal Reflection: Did I ...?

Set up my unit correctly? ☐ ☐ ☐

Slice the chicken evenly? ☐ ☐ ☐

Wash hands after preparing raw meat? ☐ ☐ ☐

Slice vegetables into even slices? ☐ ☐ ☐

Heat oil until hot? ☐ ☐ ☐

Add ingredients in the correct order? ☐ ☐ ☐

Use the right cooking times for each ingredient? ☐ ☐ ☐

Have moist chicken? ☐ ☐ ☐

Have vegetables that were al dente? ☐ ☐ ☐

Cook the pasta until al dente? ☐ ☐ ☐

Have a well-flavoured end product? ☐ ☐ ☐

Serve the dish attractively? ☐ ☐ ☐

Keep a tidy and well-organised unit throughout? ☐ ☐ ☐

Prepare, serve and clean within the time available? ☐ ☐ ☐

Q2. Evaluate your dish using the following headings:

COLOUR _____

_____

FLAVOUR _____

_____

TEXTURE _____

_____

CRITICAL FRIEND _____

_____

Q3. Based on your evaluation of the colour, flavour and texture and the comments of your critical friend, identify any changes you would make to your paprika chicken.

_____

_____

_____

_____

Q4. List two effects of cooking on meat.

Effect 1: _____

_____

Effect 2: _____

_____

Q5. Optional activity: Identify two modifications you could make to the ingredients list to help keep the dish in line with Healthy Eating Guidelines.

Healthy Eating Guideline	Modification
1.	
2.	

Q6. Optional activity: In small groups, research one of the following topics. Prepare a short summary of your research for the rest of the class.

Investigate the nutritive and dietetic value of chicken.	Research recipes that can be made using leftover chicken.	Research guidelines to follow for buying and storing both fresh and frozen chicken.
Research guidelines to follow when cooking chicken that has been frozen.	Give one reason for including chicken in the diets of the following people: an older person; a person who is on a weight-loss diet; a young child.	Research guidelines to follow when preparing and cooking chicken.

34 Spaghetti Bolognese

Learning Intentions

☆ Demonstrate the correct culinary techniques required to prepare and cook this dish.

☆ Apply appropriate hygiene and safety rules when making this dish.

☆ Evaluate the sensory attributes of this dish and its contribution to a healthy diet.

Serves: 3–4   50 mins

In a one-hour class, omit the cooking of the spaghetti.

Ingredients

1 onion

4 cloves garlic

1 red pepper

1 carrot

2 tbsp oil

400 g minced beef

400 g tin chopped tomatoes

2 tbsp tomato purée

250 g passata

1 tsp basil

1 tsp mixed herbs

1 tsp sugar

salt and pepper

250 g spaghetti

grated parmesan cheese and fresh parsley (to garnish)

If you would like to include more vegetables, sliced mushrooms or half a grated courgette are suitable options.

Equipment

Chopping board(s) (colour-coded), sharp knife, peeler, grater, garlic crusher, wooden spoon, tin opener, two large saucepans, colander, serving dishes, cutlery, two large plates (for cutlery).

Method

1. HANDS, APRON, EQUIPMENT and SET UP UNIT.

2. Weigh and measure all ingredients.

3. Peel and dice the onion. Peel and crush the garlic. Wash, deseed and dice the pepper. Peel and grate the carrot.

4. Heat one tablespoon of oil in a large saucepan. Reduce the heat and add the onion and garlic. Cook for 3–4 mins until the onion is soft.

5. Increase the heat and add the minced beef. Fry until it has turned completely brown.

6. Add the pepper and carrot and cook for a further 2 mins. If using courgette and/or mushrooms (diced), add them at this point and cook for a further 2 mins.

7. Add the chopped tomatoes, tomato purée, passata, basil, mixed herbs, sugar, salt and pepper. Bring to the boil, reduce the temperature, cover the pot and simmer for 20 mins.

8. Place the spaghetti in a saucepan of boiling water with a pinch of salt and a tablespoon of oil. Cook for 10–12 mins, then strain using a colander.

9. To serve, pour the Bolognese over the spaghetti. Garnish with grated parmesan cheese and fresh parsley.

TOP TIP

A slow cooker can be invaluable to busy families. This recipe is ideal for cooking in the slow cooker. Find out how you can adapt the recipe to do this.

TOP TIP

In busy homes, smart cooking is essential. Lasagna or cottage pie can also be made using this recipe – just double the quantity of ingredients and prepare alongside the spaghetti Bolognese. This is a clever way of having dinner prepared for the following day.

Evaluation

Date of Practical: _____

Q1. Personal Reflection: Did I ...?

Set up my unit correctly? ☐ ☐ ☐

Wash hands after preparing raw meat? ☐ ☐ ☐

Prepare vegetables as necessary? ☐ ☐ ☐

Heat oil until hot? ☐ ☐ ☐

Add ingredients in the correct order? ☐ ☐ ☐

Simmer the Bolognese for the correct length of time? ☐ ☐ ☐

Add the spaghetti to a pot of boiling water? ☐ ☐ ☐

Have a well-flavoured end product? ☐ ☐ ☐

Serve the dish attractively? ☐ ☐ ☐

Keep a tidy and well-organised unit throughout? ☐ ☐ ☐

Prepare, serve and clean within the time available? ☐ ☐ ☐

Q2. Evaluate your dish using the following headings:

COLOUR _____

_____

FLAVOUR _____

_____

TEXTURE _____

_____

CRITICAL FRIEND _____

_____

Q3. Based on your evaluation of the colour, flavour and texture and the comments of your critical friend, identify any changes you would make to your spaghetti Bolognese.

_____
_____
_____
_____
_____
_____
_____

Q4. State the advantages of putting a pinch of salt and a tablespoon of oil in the pot of boiling water when cooking pasta.

_____
_____
_____

Q5. Optional activity: **Red meat is rich in iron and is invaluable in the diet to prevent anaemia.**

What is anaemia?

_____
_____

What are the effects of anaemia on the body?

_____
_____

Q6. Optional activity: **Spaghetti Bolognese is an example of a popular dish associated with Italy. In the box below, fill in two popular dishes associated with each of the following countries:**

Country	Associated dishes
India	
Ireland	
Spain	
Mexico	
Thailand	

35 Chilli Two-Ways

Chilli Con Carne

Serves: 3   **50 mins**

In a one-hour class, omit the cooking of the rice.

Ingredients

1 small onion

2 cloves garlic

1 green pepper

1 tbsp olive oil

300 g minced meat

1 tin chopped tomatoes

1 tbsp tomato purée

2 tsp hot chilli powder (reduce if you prefer a milder taste)

1 tsp sugar

200 g red kidney beans

1 tsp cumin powder

1 tsp cayenne pepper

1 tsp cinnamon

salt and pepper

200 g rice (as accompaniment)

fresh parsley (to garnish)

guacamole and sour cream to serve as an extra accompaniment

Equipment

Chopping board(s) (colour-coded), sharp knife, garlic crusher, tin opener, wooden spoon, two saucepans, serving dishes, cutlery, two large plates (for cutlery).

Method

1. HANDS, APRON, EQUIPMENT and SET UP UNIT.

2. Weigh and measure all ingredients.

3. Peel and dice the onion. Peel and crush the garlic. Wash, deseed and dice the pepper.

4. Heat the oil in a large saucepan and fry the onion until just soft. Add the garlic and pepper and stir-fry for 2 mins.

5. Add the mince and fry it until it has turned completely brown.

6. Add the remaining ingredients: chopped tomatoes, purée, chilli powder, sugar, kidney beans, cumin powder, cayenne pepper, cinnamon and salt and pepper.

7. Bring to the boil, then reduce the temperature, cover the saucepan and simmer for 20 mins.

8. Put the rice on to cook. (See Recipe 30 for details on how to prepare and cook rice.)

9. Serve the chilli con carne with rice and garnish with fresh parsley.

Beef Tacos

TOP TIP

Chilli can be served in a variety of ways such as on top of nachos, chips or even in a wrap. Experiment!

Serves: 4

45 mins

Perfect dish for all class lengths.

Ingredients

1 small onion

2 cloves garlic

1 green pepper

1 tbsp oil

300 g minced beef

2 tsp chilli powder

2 tbsp tomato paste

1 tsp cayenne pepper

100 g sweetcorn

200 g black beans/kidney beans

110 ml boiling water

1 beef stock cube

4 hard taco shells

100 g grated cheese

TO SERVE:
guacamole, salsa, sour cream and grated cheese

Equipment

Chopping board(s) (colour-coded), sharp knife, garlic crusher, wooden spoon, heavy-based frying pan, serving dishes, cutlery, two large plates (for cutlery).

Method

1. HANDS, APRON, EQUIPMENT and SET UP UNIT.

2. Weigh and measure all ingredients.

3. Preheat the oven to 180°C/gas mark 4.

4. Top and tail, peel and dice the onion.

5. Peel and crush the garlic.

6. Wash, deseed and slice the pepper.

7. Heat the oil in a pan, add the onion and garlic and cook until the onion is soft.

8. Add the mince and cook until brown.

9. Add the chilli powder, tomato paste, cayenne pepper, sweetcorn, black beans/kidney beans and water and cook for 2–3 mins. Crumble in the stock cube, stir through gently, bring to a gentle simmer, cover the pan and simmer for 10–12 mins.

10. Place the taco shells on a baking tray. Bake for 3 mins. Alternatively heat in the microwave for 30 seconds.

11. Spoon the chilli mixture into the taco shells. Scatter some grated cheese over each.

12. Serve with guacamole, salsa and sour cream. Look back at Recipe 12 for how to make guacamole and salsa.

Evaluation

Date of Practical: _____

Q1. Personal Reflection: Did I ...?

Set up my unit correctly? ☐ ☐ ☐

Wash hands after preparing raw meat? ☐ ☐ ☐

Prepare vegetables as necessary? ☐ ☐ ☐

Heat oil until hot? ☐ ☐ ☐

Add ingredients in the correct order? ☐ ☐ ☐

Use the right cooking times for each ingredient? ☐ ☐ ☐

Prepare an accompaniment for the chilli dish (rice/taco shells/ guacamole/salsa)? ☐ ☐ ☐

Have a well-flavoured end product? ☐ ☐ ☐

Serve the dish attractively? ☐ ☐ ☐

Keep a tidy and well-organised unit throughout? ☐ ☐ ☐

Prepare, serve and clean within the time available? ☐ ☐ ☐

Q2. Evaluate your dish using the following headings:

COLOUR _____

_____

FLAVOUR _____

_____

TEXTURE _____

_____

CRITICAL FRIEND _____

_____

Q3. Based on your evaluation of the colour, flavour and texture and the comments of your critical friend, identify any changes you would make to your chilli dishes.

_____
_____
_____
_____
_____
_____
_____

Q4. Identify where you applied specific hygiene and safety rules in the preparation and serving of this dish.

HYGIENE _____

_____

_____

SAFETY _____

_____

_____

Q5. Optional activity: Plan a three-course main meal with one of the above chilli dishes as the main course. Ensure this menu is balanced (three food groups).

MENU

Starter

Main Course and Drink

Dessert

Balanced Food Check

Fruit/Veg
☐

Breads/Cereals
☐

Dairy
☐

Meat/Alternatives
☐

Q6. Optional activity: Chilli is a dish that can be served in many different ways.

(a) Find a picture in a food magazine or online of different ways in which chilli can be cooked and served.

(b) As a class, form a collage of these pictures or form your own individual collage.

(c) Display this collage on the Home Economics notice board.

36 Meatballs in Spicy Tomato Sauce

Serves: 4   **45 mins**

Perfect dish for all class lengths.

Ingredients

FOR THE SAUCE:

½ onion

3 cloves garlic

1 fresh chilli/tsp chilli flakes

2 tbsp olive oil

1 tin tomatoes

2 tbsp tomato purée

pinch salt and pepper

1 tsp sugar

FOR THE MEATBALLS:

400 g minced meat (normally beef is used but turkey/pork/lamb are also suitable)

50 g mozzarella

1 egg

½ onion

salt and pepper

2 tbsp plain flour

200 g pasta

fresh basil (for the sauce and to garnish)

Equipment

Chopping board(s) (colour-coded), sharp knife, garlic crusher, tin opener, grater, two large saucepans, frying pan, mixing bowl, wooden spoon, colander, cutlery, two large plates (for cutlery).

Method

1. HANDS, APRON, EQUIPMENT and SET UP UNIT.

2. *To make the sauce:* Top and tail, peel, halve and finely dice one onion. Peel and crush the garlic. Deseed the chilli and chop finely. Heat half the oil in a saucepan and sauté the garlic and half the onion for 3 mins. Add the tin of tomatoes, tomato purée, salt, pepper and sugar. Bring it to the boil and simmer for 15 mins.

3. *To make the meatball mixture:* Grate the mozzarella. Lightly beat the egg. Mix these with the meat and the other half of the diced onion and salt and pepper in a large bowl.

4. *To make the meatballs:* Roll a tablespoon of meatball mixture into a ball and then roll this in the flour. Repeat until all the mixture is used.

5. Heat the remaining oil in the frying pan. Gently brown the meatballs – tossing them with two spoons will help.

6. Add the browned meatballs into the simmering sauce. Continue to cook the meatballs gently in the sauce for another 15 mins.

7. Boil the pasta for 10–12 mins until al dente.

8. Chop the basil and put half into the sauce.

9. Strain the pasta in the colander.

10. Serve the meatballs on top of the pasta with the remaining basil as a garnish.

> **TOP TIP**
>
> This meatball mxture could be shaped into burger patties for a summer barbeque. Always try to adapt your favourite recipes to make other meals.

Evaluation

Date of Practical: _____

Q1. Personal Reflection: Did I ...?

Set up my unit correctly? ☐ ☐ ☐

Use my knife safely? ☐ ☐ ☐

Wash hands after preparing raw meat? ☐ ☐ ☐

Dice onions finely? ☐ ☐ ☐

Heat oil until hot? ☐ ☐ ☐

Sauté onions and garlic until softened? ☐ ☐ ☐

Make even-sized meatballs? ☐ ☐ ☐

Brown the meatballs evenly? ☐ ☐ ☐

Cook meat thoroughly? ☐ ☐ ☐

Have a well-flavoured end product? ☐ ☐ ☐

Serve the dish attractively? ☐ ☐ ☐

Keep a tidy and well-organised unit throughout? ☐ ☐ ☐

Prepare, serve and clean within the time available? ☐ ☐ ☐

Q2. Evaluate your dish using the following headings:

COLOUR _____
_____

FLAVOUR _____
_____

TEXTURE _____
_____

CRITICAL FRIEND _____
_____

Q3. Based on your evaluation of the colour, flavour and texture and the comments of your critical friend, identify any changes you would make to your meatballs.

_____

_____

_____

_____

Q4. Identify where you applied specific hygiene and safety rules in the preparation and serving of this dish.

HYGIENE _____

_____

_____

SAFETY _____

_____

_____

Q5. Optional activity: Identify some modifications you would make to the ingredients list to suit the following diets:

Special diet	Modifications
Lacto-vegetarian	
Convalescent	
Coeliac	
Pregnant woman	

Q6. Optional activity: Fresh chilli is an ingredient in this dish. In pairs, research one of the following topics. Prepare a short summary of your research for the rest of the class.

Find out the different types of fresh chilli.	What are the safety considerations when preparing a fresh chilli?	What is the hottest fresh chilli available?
How does chilli affect your taste buds?	Name two specific health benefits of chilli.	What is the country of origin of fresh chillies available in our supermarkets?

37 Steak Sandwich

Serves: 2

40 mins

In a one-hour class, this steak sandwich can be prepared, cooked and served. For a 1 hr 20 min practical class, this dish could be adapted and served as steak and wedges.

Ingredients

1 medium-sized steak (fillet, striploin, ribeye, sirloin)

2 cloves garlic

6–8 closed cup mushrooms

1 small/medium red/white onion

1 green pepper

1 tbsp olive oil

1 tbsp butter

1 tsp rosemary

1 tsp thyme

1 tsp soy sauce

2 ciabatta

2 handfuls rocket

salt and pepper to taste

FOR THE MARIE ROSE SAUCE:

2 tbsp mayonnaise

1 tbsp ketchup

2 drops tabasco sauce

Equipment

Chopping board(s) (colour-coded), sharp knife, garlic crusher, large plate, large frying pan, tongs, two serving plates, cutlery, two large plates (for cutlery).

Method

1. HANDS, APRON, EQUIPMENT and SET UP UNIT.

2. *To make the Marie Rose sauce:* Mix mayonnaise, ketchup and tabasco together. Place in fridge.

3. Remove the steak from the fridge and slice into thin strips, cutting across the grain.

4. Peel and crush the garlic.

5. Wash the mushrooms gently and pat dry using kitchen paper. Chop the mushrooms. Peel and finely slice the onion. Wash, deseed and slice the green pepper.

6. Heat the olive oil in a large frying pan over a medium heat.

7. Add the butter, crushed garlic, rosemary and thyme, place the steak in the pan and cook for 3–5 mins until brown.

8. Add the mushrooms, onions, green pepper and soy sauce to the pan and cook for 3–5 mins, stirring occasionally until cooked. The meat should be cooked through and moist at this stage. Add some cracked black pepper and salt to taste.

9. Slice each ciabatta in two. Grill under a medium heat until lightly browned or place in a pop-up toaster and toast.

10. *To assemble:* Add a handful of rocket to each ciabatta and divide the steak and vegetable mixture between each. Serve with the Marie Rose sauce.

TOP TIP

Steak is a very popular dish, but it can be an expensive. It is important to remember that cheaper cuts of meat can be as flavoursome and are just as nutritious. When buying meat, don't be afraid to ask the butcher's advice on which cut is best value and how to cook it. My father, Marty Fallon, was a butcher with a great knowledge and understanding of how best to prepare, cook and serve the different cuts of meat. He loved to share his knowledge with his customers. The next time you are at the meat counter and have a question about a recipe or a cut of meat, just ask the butcher!

Evaluation

Date of Practical: _____

Q1. Personal Reflection: Did I ...?

Set up my unit correctly? ☐ ☐ ☐

Wash hands after preparing raw meat? ☐ ☐ ☐

Slice mushrooms and onions evenly? ☐ ☐ ☐

Wash the pepper and slice it evenly? ☐ ☐ ☐

Heat oil until hot? ☐ ☐ ☐

Add ingredients in the correct order? ☐ ☐ ☐

Have moist meat? ☐ ☐ ☐

Have a well-flavoured end product? ☐ ☐ ☐

Serve the dish attractively? ☐ ☐ ☐

Keep a tidy and well-organised unit throughout? ☐ ☐ ☐

Prepare, serve and clean within the time available? ☐ ☐ ☐

Q2. Evaluate your dish using the following headings:

COLOUR _____

_____

FLAVOUR _____

_____

TEXTURE _____

_____

CRITICAL FRIEND _____

_____

Q3. Based on your evaluation of the colour, flavour and texture and the comments of your critical friend, identify any changes you would make to your steak sandwich.

_____

_____

_____

_____

_____

_____

_____

Q4. The steak in this recipe is fried. Name an alternative cooking method that could be used to prepare and cook the steak. Explain an advantage of using this alternative cooking method.

Alternative cooking method:

_____

Advantage:

_____

_____

_____

Q5. Optional activity: Identify some modifications you would make to the ingredients list or cooking methods to suit the following diets:

Diet	Modifications
Vegan	
Low cholesterol	

Q6. Optional activity: Cheaper cuts of meat are just as nutritious as more expensive cuts of meat. Plan two three-course main meals suitable for a family on a budget. The main course must contain a cheaper cut of meat. Ensure the menu is balanced (three food groups).

MENU

Starter

Main Course and Drink

Dessert

Balanced Food Check

Fruit/Veg
☐

Breads/Cereals
☐

Dairy
☐

Meat/Alternatives
☐

MENU

Starter

Main Course and Drink

Dessert

Balanced Food Check

Fruit/Veg
☐

Breads/Cereals
☐

Dairy
☐

Meat/Alternatives
☐

UNIT 6
Fish

38. FISH IN A BAG

39. LAYERED FISH BAKE

40. THAI GREEN PRAWN CURRY

41. ZESTY POLENTA-CRUSTED FISH CAKES

38 Fish in a Bag

Serves: 2   **45 mins**

Perfect dish for all class lengths.

Ingredients

small knob fresh root ginger

1 clove garlic

zest and juice of 1 lemon/lime

2 tbsp soy sauce

2 VEGETABLE CHOICES FROM THE FOLLOWING:

10 baby corn

4 spring onions

12 mange tout

1 carrot

½ courgette

6 cherry tomatoes

2 fish fillets (choose in-season)

TO SERVE:

10 baby potatoes/200 g brown rice

TOP TIP

Ask your fishmonger to recommend value-for-money fish. Shellfish such as prawns add a touch of class to these fish parcels – perhaps your fishmonger will give you a good bargain!

Equipment

Chopping board(s) (colour-coded), sharp knife, grater, garlic crusher, juicer, two sheets of tin foil, baking tray, fish slice, cutlery, two large plates (for cutlery).

Learning Intentions

☆ Choose ingredients to make a colourful and attractive meal.

☆ Apply appropriate hygiene and safety rules when making this dish.

☆ Use a variety of preparation and cooking techniques to make this dish.

☆ Demonstrate creative skills in serving this dish attractively.

☆ Evaluate the sensory attributes of this dish and its contribution to a healthy diet.

Method

1. HANDS, APRON, EQUIPMENT and SET UP UNIT.

2. Preheat the oven to 180°C/gas mark 4.

3. Peel and grate the ginger, peel and crush the garlic.

4. Wash and zest the lemon/lime using the fine side of the grater, only removing the skin and being careful not to grate down to the pith. Halve the lemon/lime and juice using the juicer.

5. Mix the ginger, garlic, juice, zest and soy sauce together.

6. Wash and prepare the vegetables: halve and quarter the baby corn lengthways, top and tail, cut into 3 cm pieces and then halve the spring onion, peel and julienne the carrot, cut the courgette into thin circles and halve the cherry tomatoes.

7. Place the fish fillets on a chopping board. Check for bones by running your finger over the fillet. (They're unlikely to be there but if there are any bones they are easy to find in the raw fish!) If you find any, pull them out with your fingers or a cook's tweezers.

8. Put a large square of tin foil, shiny side up, on the baking tray. Put the fish in the middle of the tin foil. Arrange all the vegetables on top. Pour over half the sauce.

9. Fold both sides of the tin foil up to envelop the fish. Make a double fold at each end to seal completely and pinch or scrunch the ends to ensure the fish is sealed in and no liquid can seep out. Make sure that the parcel isn't too tight, however, so air can circulate within the parcel.

10. Repeat this process with the second piece of fish, remaining vegetables and sauce.

11. Bake in the oven for 15 mins.

12. Boil the potatoes for 8–10 mins until tender/Put the rice on to cook. (See Recipe 30 for details on how to prepare and cook rice.)

13. Remove the fish from the oven. Carefully open the top of the fish parcel, as steam will escape when you open it, which can cause a nasty burn. If the skin comes away easily from the fillet, it is cooked.

14. Carefully remove from the bag using a fish slice and garnish with fresh herbs or a wedge of lemon.

15. Serve beside the potatoes/rice.

Evaluation

Date of Practical: _____

Q1. Personal Reflection: Did I ...?

Set up my unit correctly? ☐ ☐ ☐

Use my knife safely? ☐ ☐ ☐

Use the grater safely? ☐ ☐ ☐

Ensure fish is bone-free? ☐ ☐ ☐

Wash hands after preparing raw fish? ☐ ☐ ☐

Slice vegetables finely and evenly? ☐ ☐ ☐

Seal the fish parcels completely? ☐ ☐ ☐

Cook fish until it is flaking away from the skin? ☐ ☐ ☐

Have a well-flavoured end product? ☐ ☐ ☐

Serve the dish attractively? ☐ ☐ ☐

Keep a tidy and well-organised unit throughout? ☐ ☐ ☐

Prepare, serve and clean within the time available? ☐ ☐ ☐

Q2. Evaluate your dish using the following headings:

COLOUR _____

_____

FLAVOUR _____

_____

TEXTURE _____

_____

CRITICAL FRIEND _____

_____

Q3. Based on your evaluation of the colour, flavour and texture and the comments of your critical friend, identify any changes you would make to your fish in a bag dish.

_____

_____

_____

_____

_____

_____

_____

_____

Q4. The fish parcels are sealed so the contents inside are steamed. State two advantages of steaming as a cooking method.

Advantage 1:

_____

_____

Advantage 2:

_____

_____

Q5. Optional activity: **Fish does not contain any carbohydrates or vitamin C, so it should be served with foods containing these nutrients to ensure the meal is balanced. In relation to the ingredients you chose for this dish, identify if and where you have included these nutrients:**

Nutrient	Included/Not Included
Carbohydrate	
Vitamin C	

Q6. Optional activity: **Irish organic salmon is considered to be a premium product worldwide. Bord Iascaigh Mhara states that Irish salmon are 'only fed a diet of sustainable organic feed' and that they are raised 'in more spacious pens than traditional farmed salmon'.**

(a) Working in pairs and drawing on your knowledge of sustainability in the food industry, explain what you understand by the following three terms: organic salmon; sustainable organic feed; farmed salmon.

(b) Looking at this label, state the origin of this fish:

_____

39 Layered Fish Bake

Serves: 4

50 mins

Perfect dish for all class lengths.

Equipment

Chopping board(s) (colour-coded), sharp knife, tin opener, medium-sized casserole dish, saucepan, grater, mixing bowl, wooden spoon, oven gloves, cutlery, two large plates (for cutlery).

Ingredients

2 fillets (380 g) of any type of white fish

1 medium onion

1 medium carrot

½ courgette

1 yellow/green bell pepper

3 cloves garlic

1 tbsp olive oil

1 tin chopped tomatoes

2 tsp mixed herbs

salt and pepper

100 g grated cheese

60 g breadcrumbs

fresh parsley (to garnish)

180 g prawns (optional)

POSSIBLE ACCOMPANIMENT:

This dish can be served with a green summer salad or boiled baby potatoes and broccoli.

Method

1. HANDS, APRON, EQUIPMENT and SET UP UNIT.

2. Preheat the oven to 180°C/gas mark 4.

3. Weigh and measure all ingredients.

4. Peel and chop the onion. Peel and grate the carrot. Peel the courgette into ribbons (using a vegetable peeler). Wash, deseed and slice the pepper. Peel and crush the garlic.

5. Grease the casserole dish, place the ribbons of courgette in it, then place the fish on top of the courgette, skin-side down.

6. Heat the oil in a saucepan on a medium setting and cook the onion for 1–2 mins until soft. Add the chopped tomatoes, garlic, carrot, yellow/green bell pepper and mixed herbs. Add salt and pepper to taste.

7. Simmer for 5–6 mins on a medium heat.

8. Grate the cheese and mix together with the breadcrumbs.

9. Pour the tomato mixture over the fish in the casserole dish and bake for 10 mins. (If using the prawns, place them on top of the fish before adding the tomato mixture.)

10. Sprinkle the grated cheese and breadcrumb mixture over the top and then bake for a further 20 mins until crisp.

11. Remove from the oven using oven gloves and serve hot. Garnish with fresh parsley.

TOP TIP

It is important to remember when buying fresh fish that some varieties such as pollock and ling can be just as tasty if not nicer than cod, and at a greatly reduced price. This also helps with the sustainability and viability of cod stocks in the Atlantic Ocean.

Evaluation

Date of Practical: _____

Q1. Personal Reflection: Did I ...?

Set up my unit correctly? ☐ ☐ ☐

Preheat the oven to correct temperature? ☐ ☐ ☐

Prepare vegetables as necessary? ☐ ☐ ☐

Heat oil until hot? ☐ ☐ ☐

Simmer the tomato sauce for the correct length of time? ☐ ☐ ☐

Assemble the bake in the correct order? ☐ ☐ ☐

Cook for the correct length of time? ☐ ☐ ☐

Have a well-flavoured end product? ☐ ☐ ☐

Keep a tidy and well-organised unit throughout? ☐ ☐ ☐

Prepare, serve and clean within the time available? ☐ ☐ ☐

Q2. Evaluate your dish using the following headings:

COLOUR _____

_____

FLAVOUR _____

_____

TEXTURE _____

_____

CRITICAL FRIEND _____

_____

Q3. Based on your evaluation of the colour, flavour and texture and the comments of your critical friend, identify any changes you would make to your layered fish bake.

_____

_____

_____

_____

_____

_____

_____

_____

Q4. Fish is the main ingredient in this dish. It has been baked. Name three other ways of cooking fish.

1. _____

2. _____

3. _____

Q5. Optional activity: **White fish is a nutritious food. Evaluate the nutritional and dietetic contribution of white fish to our diet. Include four points of information.**

Nutrient	Value to the diet

Q6. Optional activity: **In small groups, research one of the following topics. Prepare a short summary of your research for the rest of the class.**

List the classes of fish, giving three examples for each. Explain the following cuts of fish: whole fish; fish fillet; fish steak.	Plan a three-course menu that includes fish. Remember to do your balanced-food check!	List the guidelines to follow when buying fresh fish.
List the ways in which fish can be preserved. Include examples of popular types of fish that have been preserved using each method.	List the guidelines for storing fresh and frozen fish.	Research and list ways of including fish as part of a healthy breakfast or lunch.

40 Thai Green Prawn Curry

Learning Intentions

☆ Demonstrate the correct culinary techniques required to prepare and cook this dish.

☆ Apply appropriate hygiene and safety rules when making this dish.

☆ Evaluate the sensory attributes of this dish and its contribution to a healthy diet.

Serves: 3–4   35 mins

Perfect dish for all class lengths.

Ingredients

1 red chilli

stalk fresh lemongrass

1 lime

1 tbsp olive oil

2 tbsp Thai green curry paste

400 ml tin coconut milk

1 tbsp fish sauce/soya sauce

1 tbsp brown sugar

400 g raw peeled king prawns

3–5 VEGETABLE CHOICES FROM THE FOLLOWING:

60 g baby corn

60g mange tout

1 pak choi

100 g broccoli florets

1 red/green pepper

100 g frozen peas

small bunch fresh coriander (optional)

POSSIBLE ACCOMPANIMENT:
300 g rice (noodles are also a suitable option)

Equipment

Chopping board(s) (colour-coded), sharp knife, peeler, grater, garlic crusher, wooden spoon, wok/frying pan, saucepan, colander, serving plates, cutlery, two large plates (for cutlery).

Method

1. HANDS, APRON, EQUIPMENT and SET UP UNIT.

2. Weigh and measure all ingredients.

3. Wash and finely slice the chilli. Discard the outer layer of the lemongrass and slice finely. Halve and juice the lime.

4. Slice the baby corn in two lengthways. Wash and slice the mange tout in two lengthways. Cut off the root end of the pak choi and slice.

5. Wash the broccoli. Cut the florets from the head of broccoli into bite-sized pieces. Wash the pepper, deseed and slice thinly.

6. Put the rice on to cook. (See Recipe 30 for details on how to prepare and cook rice.)

7. Heat the oil in a wok or large frying pan on a medium heat and add the curry paste. Fry for 2 mins.

8. Pour in the lime juice, coconut milk, fish sauce and brown sugar. Bring to the boil and reduce to a simmer. Add the prawns, chilli and chosen vegetables. Gently simmer for 5 mins or until the prawns are cooked through. The vegetables should be al dente.

9. Remove the pan or wok from the heat and stir through finely sliced coriander.

10. Serve over a bed of rice/noodles and sprinkle with some coriander leaves.

TOP TIP

Deseed the chillies to remove some of the heat from the dish. Chicken can also be used in this dish, as an alternative to prawns, or for an extra luxurious dish you can use both! If using chicken, add in with the curry paste and fry until white before adding the coconut milk.

Evaluation

Date of Practical: _____

Q1. Personal Reflection: Did I ...?

Set up my unit correctly? ☐ ☐ ☐

Slice vegetables evenly? ☐ ☐ ☐

Use my knife safely? ☐ ☐ ☐

Heat oil until hot? ☐ ☐ ☐

Add ingredients in the correct order? ☐ ☐ ☐

Use the right cooking times for each ingredient? ☐ ☐ ☐

Have vegetables that were al dente? ☐ ☐ ☐

Cook rice until fluffy? ☐ ☐ ☐

Have a well-flavoured end product? ☐ ☐ ☐

Keep a tidy and well-organised unit throughout? ☐ ☐ ☐

Prepare, serve and clean within the time available? ☐ ☐ ☐

Q2. Evaluate your dish using the following headings:

COLOUR _____

_____

FLAVOUR _____

_____

TEXTURE _____

_____

CRITICAL FRIEND _____

_____

Q3. Based on your evaluation of the colour, flavour and texture and the comments of your critical friend, identify any changes you would make to your Thai green prawn curry.

_____

_____

_____

_____

_____

_____

_____

_____

Q4. Many curries are cooked using the gentle cooking method of stewing. Define 'stewing' and suggest two guidelines to follow when stewing foods.

Definition: _____

_____

Guideline 1: _____

_____

Guideline 2: _____

_____

Q5. Optional activity: Prawns are a type of shellfish. In the box, identify two types of fish belonging to each category:

White fish	Oily fish	Shellfish
1.	1.	1.
2.	2.	2.

Explain two nutritional benefits of including fish in the diet:

Benefit 1:	
Benefit 2:	

Q6. Optional activity: Thailand is famous for its curries. Investigate the difference between Thai red curry, Thai green curry and Thai yellow curry. Include details on the colour of the chillies used, which curry is hottest and which is spiciest.

Thai red curry	
Thai green curry	
Thai yellow curry	

41 Zesty Polenta-Crusted Fish Cakes

Equipment

Chopping board(s) (colour-coded), sharp knife, weighing scales, two medium-sized saucepans, grater/zester, juicer, peeler, potato masher, frying pan/baking tray, cutlery, two large plates (for cutlery).

Method

1. HANDS, APRON, EQUIPMENT and SET UP UNIT.
2. Preheat the oven to 180°C/gas mark 4.
3. Using the peeler, peel the potatoes. Chop each potato into approximately eight equal-sized chunks.
4. Add the potatoes to boiling water and boil for 8–10 mins until the potatoes are tender when a knife is inserted. Strain the water. Turn the hob off and allow the potatoes to steam with the lid on for a few minutes (to dry them out fully) before mashing. Mash the potatoes with a masher.
5. Add the milk and the fish to a saucepan. Bring to the boil and then reduce the heat to a poaching temperature. Poach the fish until it flakes easily from the skin (4–7 mins depending on size).
6. Wash and zest the lemon and lime using the fine side of the grater, only removing the skin and being careful not to grate down to the pith. Halve and juice the lemon/lime using the juicer.
7. Top and tail the scallion/chives and chop into tiny circles.
8. Wash the coriander, make a chiffonade and slice into small pieces. (Look back to Recipe 12 to remind yourself of the chiffonade technique.)
9. Remove fish from the poaching liquid. Flake it away from the skin in large chunks.
10. While the fish is cooling, crack the egg into a small bowl and beat gently.
11. Add potato, zest, juice, pepper and egg into a mixing bowl. Mix vigorously to combine all ingredients evenly.
12. Add the chunks of fish. Combine gently to avoid breaking the fish.
13. Sprinkle half the polenta/breadcrumbs onto the baking tray and form six even-sized cakes on top of the polenta/breadcrumbs. (It is easier to form them directly on the baking tray instead of having to move them.) Use your hands to coat the sides of the fish cakes with the polenta/breadcrumbs and then sprinkle the top of the fish cake with the remaining polenta/breadcrumbs.
14. Drizzle with oil and bake for 15–20 mins until browned evenly.
15. Serve with a salad such as Recipe 48 Summer Salad with Citrus Dressing to make this a complete meal.

Learning Intentions

★ Use a variety of preparation and cooking techniques to make this dish.

★ Apply appropriate hygiene and safety rules when making this dish.

★ Demonstrate the correct culinary techniques required to prepare and cook this dish.

★ Evaluate the sensory attributes of this dish and its contribution to a healthy diet.

★ Evaluate the cost of fish in the diet of a low-income family.

Makes: 6 fish cakes　　**50 mins**

Perfect dish for all class lengths.

Ingredients

5 medium potatoes

150 ml milk

500 g salmon/450 g white fish plus 50 g smoked fish (for extra flavour)

zest of lemon

zest of lime

2–3 tbsp lemon/lime juice

1 tbsp scallion/chives

2 tbsp coriander

1 egg

freshly ground black pepper

100 g polenta/breadcrumbs

olive oil (for cooking)

TOP TIP

In order to follow Healthy Eating Guidelines, the fish cakes in this recipe are baked. However, they can be fried for 3 mins on each side before baking. This makes the polenta crispier in texture.

Evaluation

Date of Practical: _____

Q1. Personal Reflection: Did I ...?

Set up my unit correctly? ☐ ☐ ☐

Boil potatoes until tender enough to mash? ☐ ☐ ☐

Poach the fish at the correct temperature? ☐ ☐ ☐

Cook the fish until it started to flake away from the skin? ☐ ☐ ☐

Zest the skin of the fruit only? ☐ ☐ ☐

Chop scallion/chives finely and evenly? ☐ ☐ ☐

Combine fish cake mixture without breaking the fish? ☐ ☐ ☐

Shape cakes into even pieces? ☐ ☐ ☐

Coat cakes evenly with polenta/breadcrumbs? ☐ ☐ ☐

Brown the fish cakes evenly? ☐ ☐ ☐

Have a well-flavoured end product? ☐ ☐ ☐

Serve the dish attractively? ☐ ☐ ☐

Keep a tidy and well-organised unit throughout? ☐ ☐ ☐

Prepare, serve and clean within the time available? ☐ ☐ ☐

Q2. Evaluate your dish using the following headings:

COLOUR _____

_____

FLAVOUR _____

_____

TEXTURE _____

_____

CRITICAL FRIEND _____

_____

Q3. Based on your evaluation of the colour, flavour and texture and the comments of your critical friend, identify any changes you would make to your fish cakes.

_____

_____

_____

_____

Q4. Define 'poaching' and suggest two guidelines to be followed when poaching foods.

Definition: _____

_____

Guideline 1: _____

_____

Guideline 2: _____

_____

Q5. Optional activity: Oily fish such as salmon has many nutritional benefits in the diet. List three groups of people who benefit from eating oily fish. State the nutritional reason why oily fish is of benefit to them.

Group who benefit from eating oily fish	Nutritional reason
1.	
2.	
3.	

Q6. Optional activity: Fish can be considered to be a high-cost food item and is sometimes eliminated from the diets of low-income families as a result.

(a) Compare two different fresh and frozen fish fillets in terms of price per 100 g.

Fish	Fresh price per 100 g	Frozen price per 100 g

(b) Using the cheapest option, calculate how much it would cost to buy this fish for a main meal for a family of four:

_____

(c) Do you consider this to be an expensive protein choice for a family?   Yes ☐   No ☐

(d) Explain your answer:

_____

_____

UNIT 7
Fruit

42. FRESH FRUIT SALAD AND FRUIT SKEWERS

43. FRUIT CRUMBLE

42 Fresh Fruit Salad and Fruit Skewers

Serves: 4   **25 mins**

Perfect dish for all class lengths.

Equipment

Chopping board(s) (colour-coded), sharp knife, peeler, orange juice squeezer, serving bowl, cutlery, two large plates (for cutlery).

TOP TIP

Any fruit can be used to make a fruit salad. If using banana, ensure the fruit salad is consumed quickly after being made. Alternatively, dip the banana in lemon juice as this will help prevent it from browning. Lemon juice also helps to prevent apples and pears from browning.

Ingredients

1 red apple

10 green grapes

10 black grapes

10 strawberries

2 mandarin oranges

2 kiwis

1 mango

2 oranges

1 tbsp lemon juice

fresh mint (to garnish)

Method

1. HANDS, APRON, EQUIPMENT and SET UP UNIT.

2. Gather ingredients.

3. Wash apple, grapes and strawberries.

4. Core apple and cut it into even-sized slices. Dip in lemon juice. Place in serving bowl.

5. Halve the grapes lengthways and remove seeds. Place in serving bowl.

6. Remove the strawberry stem from each strawberry. Cut each strawberry in two lengthways. Place in serving bowl.

7. Peel mandarin oranges, divide into segments and remove any obvious white membrane. Place in the serving bowl.

8. Peel kiwis with a vegetable peeler. Slice and place in serving bowl.

9. Peel and chop the mango (around the stone) into even-sized pieces and place in the serving bowl.

10. Cut both oranges in half. Using a juice squeezer, squeeze each half. Pour the juice into a jug.

11. Gently stir the fruit ingredients. Pour the freshly squeezed orange juice over them.

12. Garnish with a sprig of mint.

Fruit Skewers

Fruit skewers are a colourful, interesting and fun way of presenting fruit. The novelty of fruit skewers is a good way of encouraging children to eat more fruit and are a healthy option at parties. Fruit skewers are made by threading chunks of fresh fruit onto wooden sticks or metal skewers. They can be arranged attractively on a serving plate. A dip can also be presented with the fruit skewers such as a yogurt, honey and cinnamon dip or a chocolate dip. Using the image of the fruit skewer as inspiration, design and create your own fruit skewer.

Evaluation

Date of Practical: _____

Q1. Personal Reflection: Did I ...?

Set up my unit correctly? ☐ ☐ ☐	Stir fruit gently in serving bowl? ☐ ☐ ☐
Wash the fruit? ☐ ☐ ☐	Pour orange juice over fruit? ☐ ☐ ☐
Peel the fruit as necessary? ☐ ☐ ☐	Have a colourful and attractively presented dish? ☐ ☐ ☐
Slice the fruit into even slices? ☐ ☐ ☐	Have a variety of textures in my dish? ☐ ☐ ☐
Dip the bananas/apples/pears in lemon juice to prevent browning? ☐ ☐ ☐	Keep a tidy and well-organised unit throughout? ☐ ☐ ☐
Remove seeds or stones from fruit? ☐ ☐ ☐	Prepare, serve and clean within the time available? ☐ ☐ ☐
Ensure maximum juice was gained from each half of the orange? ☐ ☐ ☐	

Q2. Evaluate your dish using the following headings:

COLOUR _____

_____

FLAVOUR _____

_____

TEXTURE _____

_____

CRITICAL FRIEND _____

_____

Q3. Based on your evaluation of the colour, flavour and texture and the comments of your critical friend, identify any changes you would make to your fruit salad/fruit skewers.

_____

_____

_____

_____

_____

_____

_____

Q4. Identify where you applied specific hygiene and safety rules in the preparation and serving of this dish.

HYGIENE _____

_____

SAFETY _____

_____

Q5. Optional activity: It is recommended that a person consumes between five and seven portions of fruit and vegetables a day. Ensuring correct portion size is an essential component of planning meals. With that in mind:

(a) Choose your four favourite fruits/vegetables to eat.

(b) Using www.safefood.eu, find out what the correct portion size is for your choices.

Favourite fruit/veg	Correct portion size
1.	
2.	
3.	
4.	

Q6. Optional activity: There are many types of fruit that cannot be grown in Ireland. In groups of three–four, discuss the following questions and then present your findings to the class:

(a) Name five fruits that cannot easily be grown in Ireland.

(b) Are there consequences to food being transported around the world? If so, what are they?

(c) Can you suggest ways of helping to reduce food miles?

Present your group's information to the rest of the class and discuss.

43 Fruit Crumble

Learning Intentions

☆ Choose ingredients to make this dish.

☆ Demonstrate the correct culinary techniques required to prepare and cook this dish.

☆ Apply appropriate hygiene and safety rules when making this dish.

☆ Evaluate the sensory attributes of this dish and its contribution to a healthy diet.

Serves: 6 **55 mins**

In a one-hour class, reduce the number of apples used and instead use more berries or frozen fruit.

Equipment

Chopping board(s) (colour-coded), sharp knife, saucepan and lid, sieve, weighing scales, wooden spoon, mixing bowl, peeler, cutlery, pot stand, ovenproof dish/six mini ramekin dishes, oven gloves, cutlery, two large plates (for cutlery).

TOP TIP

Many different types of fruits are suitable to use in a fruit crumble. However, it is important to remember that if the fruit you are using is a sour fruit (e.g. gooseberries), more sugar will be needed to sweeten this dish. Serving fruit crumble in mini ramekin dishes is ideal for special occasions.

Ingredients

3 large cooking apples

2 tbsp water

50 g sugar

1 small punnet raspberries/

10 strawberries (alternatively a selection of frozen fruit can be used)

FOR THE CRUMBLE TOPPING:

150 g plain flour

75 g margarine/butter

50 g brown sugar

25 g porridge oats

Method

1. HANDS, APRON, EQUIPMENT and SET UP UNIT.

2. Preheat the oven to 180°C/gas mark 4.

3. Weigh and measure all ingredients. Grease the ovenproof dish or mini ramekins with a little butter/margarine.

4. Wash, peel, core and thinly slice the apples. Place them in a saucepan with the two tablespoons of water. Bring to the boil, reduce the temperature and stew for 5 mins until they are al dente.

5. Remove from the heat and stir in the sugar.

6. Pour them into the ovenproof dish/mini ramekin dishes.

7. Wash the raspberries/wash and remove the green stem of the strawberries and slice in two.

8. Place the raspberries/strawberries on top of the apple.

9. Sieve the flour into a mixing bowl.

10. Rub in the margarine/butter until it resembles breadcrumbs.

11. Stir in the sugar and porridge oats.

12. Pour the crumble on top of the apple mixture and spread evenly.

13. Bake for 30–35 mins until the fruit crumble is golden brown.

14. Remove from the oven using oven gloves and serve with custard, whipped cream or ice cream.

Evaluation

Date of Practical: _____

Q1. Personal Reflection: Did I ...?

Set up my unit correctly? ☐ ☐ ☐

Weigh ingredients correctly? ☐ ☐ ☐

Wash, peel and evenly slice the fruit? ☐ ☐ ☐

Stew apples until al dente? ☐ ☐ ☐

Rub the margarine/ butter into the flour until it resembled breadcrumbs? ☐ ☐ ☐

Assemble the dish correctly before placing in the oven? ☐ ☐ ☐

Bake until the topping was golden? ☐ ☐ ☐

Have a well-flavoured end product? ☐ ☐ ☐

Keep a tidy and well-organised unit throughout? ☐ ☐ ☐

Prepare, serve and clean within the time available? ☐ ☐ ☐

Q2. Evaluate your dish using the following headings:

COLOUR _____

_____

FLAVOUR _____

_____

TEXTURE _____

_____

CRITICAL FRIEND _____

_____

Q3. Based on your evaluation of the colour, flavour and texture and the comments of your critical friend, identify any changes you would make to your fruit crumble.

_____

_____

_____

_____

_____

_____

_____

Q4. Stewing and baking are the cooking methods used in making fruit crumble. State one advantage of stewing the apples before baking the apple crumble.

_____

_____

Q5. Optional activity: When making fruit crumble, identify two modifications that could be made to the crumble topping to contribute to its sensory attributes.

Modifications
1.
2.

Q6. Optional activity: It is important to encourage people of all ages to eat more fruit.

(a) Gather pictures from magazines or online of interesting and varied ways of including fruit in the diet. Bring the pictures to class.

(b) Form a collage of pictures showing the varied ways of including fruit in the diet. Display this collage on the Home Economics notice board.

(c) As a class, discuss the benefits of including fruit in the diet.

UNIT 8

Pulses, Vegetables and Salads

44. COCONUTTY LENTIL CURRY

45. PENNE AL'ARRABBIATA

46. WARM CHICKEN SALAD

47. CRISPY SMOKED PANCETTA AND POTATO SALAD

48. SUMMER SALAD WITH CITRUS DRESSING

44 Coconutty Lentil Curry

Learning Intentions

☆ Use a variety of preparation and cooking techniques to make this dish.

☆ Apply appropriate hygiene and safety rules when making this dish.

☆ Evaluate the sensory attributes of this dish and its contribution to a healthy diet.

Serves: 3–4   **40 mins**

In a one-hour class, omit the cooking of the rice.

Ingredients

100 g dried lentils (any colour)

400 g chickpeas (canned)

1 onion

1 green/yellow pepper

2 sweet potatoes

1 tbsp oil

2 tbsp curry powder/paste

400 ml coconut milk

1 tin tomatoes

50 g frozen peas

300 g rice

fresh coriander (to garnish)

Equipment

Chopping board(s) (colour-coded), sharp knife, sieve, tin opener, large saucepan and lid, medium-sized saucepan and lid, peeler, wooden spoon, cutlery, two large plates (for cutlery).

Method

1. HANDS, APRON, EQUIPMENT and SET UP UNIT.

2. Weigh the lentils and strain the chickpeas in the sieve.

3. Top and tail, peel and dice the onion.

4. Wash the pepper, halve and deseed it, cut into thick slices and then halve each slice into chunks.

5. Peel the sweet potatoes and chop into chunks.

6. Heat the oil in a saucepan. Add the onion, turn down the heat and sauté for 3 mins until it has softened.

7. Add the curry powder/paste and cook for 1 min.

8. Turn up the heat and add the lentils, sweet potato, coconut milk and tinned tomatoes. Bring to the boil, then simmer for 15 mins.

9. Put the rice on to cook. (See Recipe 30 for details on how to prepare and cook rice.)

10. Add the pepper to the curry and simmer for a further 5 mins.

11. Just before serving, add the chickpeas and frozen peas for long enough to heat through.

12. Serve accompanied with the rice and garnished with the chopped coriander. Naan bread would also be an excellent accompaniment.

TOP TIP

Increase iron easily in this dish by experimenting with green vegetables. Broccoli could be added at the same time as the pepper, and spinach could be added at the same time as the chickpeas and frozen peas.

Evaluation

Date of Practical: _____

Q1. Personal Reflection: Did I ...?

Set up my unit correctly? ☐ ☐ ☐

Use my knife safely? ☐ ☐ ☐

Chop vegetables evenly? ☐ ☐ ☐

Add onion to hot oil? ☐ ☐ ☐

Sauté onion gently until softened? ☐ ☐ ☐

Add ingredients in the correct sequence? ☐ ☐ ☐

Use correct temperature control throughout? ☐ ☐ ☐

Cook rice until it was fluffy? ☐ ☐ ☐

Serve the dish attractively? ☐ ☐ ☐

Have a well-flavoured end product? ☐ ☐ ☐

Keep a tidy and well-organised unit throughout? ☐ ☐ ☐

Prepare, serve and clean within the time available? ☐ ☐ ☐

Q2. Evaluate your dish using the following headings:

COLOUR _____
_____

FLAVOUR _____
_____

TEXTURE _____
_____

CRITICAL FRIEND _____
_____

Q3. Based on your evaluation of the colour, flavour and texture and the comments of your critical friend, identify any changes you would make to your coconutty lentil curry.

_____

_____

_____

_____

_____

_____

_____

_____

Q4. Identify where you applied specific hygiene and safety rules in the preparation and serving of this dish.

HYGIENE _____

_____

SAFETY _____

_____

Q5. Optional activity: Name three types of vegetarian diets. List foods that can and cannot be included when adhering to these diets. Identify whether or not this recipe is suitable for these diets.

Vegetarian diets	Foods eaten	Foods not eaten	Is this curry dish suitable?

Q6. Optional activity: A curry is a form of stew native to Asia. In Ireland today, curry is a very popular dish. List three reasons why curry has become so popular in the Irish diet:

Reason 1:

_____

_____

Reason 2:

_____

_____

Reason 3:

_____

_____

45 Penne Al'Arrabbiata

Serves: 2　　**40 mins**

Perfect dish for all class lengths.

Ingredients

1 onion

3 cloves garlic

1 chilli/1 tsp smoked paprika

1 tbsp olive oil

500 ml passata (or 1 tin tomatoes + 2 tbsp tomato purée)

1 tsp sugar

1 tbsp cream cheese (optional)

ground black pepper and salt

grated low-fat cheese/ parmesan shavings (to garnish)

200 g penne pasta

Equipment

Chopping board(s) (colour-coded), sharp knife, garlic crusher, tin opener, wooden spoon, two saucepans, colander, grater, pasta dish for serving, cutlery, two large plates (for cutlery).

Method

1. HANDS, APRON, EQUIPMENT and SET UP UNIT.

2. Weigh and measure all ingredients.

3. Peel and dice the onion very finely.

4. Peel and crush the garlic.

5. Deseed and finely chop the chilli.

6. Heat the oil in a saucepan and gently cook the onion, garlic and chilli/smoked paprika for 3 mins or until the onion has softened.

7. Add in the passata (or tomatoes and tomato purée), sugar, salt and pepper.

8. Bring to the boil, then reduce heat and simmer for 20 mins. Melt the cream cheese (if using) into the sauce after simmering.

9. Grate the low-fat cheese (if using) and leave in the fridge.

10. Bring a saucepan of water to the boil, add a pinch of salt and add the pasta. Cook until al dente (approx. 10 mins).

11. Strain the pasta in a colander.

12. Pour the pasta into the sauce and gently combine.

13. Serve on a pasta dish sprinkled with a little grated cheese/ shaved parmesan.

TOP TIP

Chorizo can be added to this dish, giving an interesting flavour and texture. If adding, this dish would require half a chorizo sausage sliced into 1 cm circles, which are added to the pan before the onion, garlic and chilli/smoked paprika. Alternatively, to keep this dish vegetarian-friendly, pine nuts could be added and are a good source of protein.

Evaluation

Date of Practical: _____

Q1. Personal Reflection: Did I ...?

Set up my unit correctly? ☐ ☐ ☐	Bring the dish to the boil after adding the passata/ tomatoes? ☐ ☐ ☐
Peel and dice onion finely? ☐ ☐ ☐	Reduce the temperature and allow the dish to simmer for 20 mins? ☐ ☐ ☐
Peel and crush garlic? ☐ ☐ ☐	
Deseed and finely chop the chilli? ☐ ☐ ☐	Have pasta that was al dente? ☐ ☐ ☐
Heat oil until hot? ☐ ☐ ☐	Have a well-flavoured end product? ☐ ☐ ☐
Add ingredients in the correct order? ☐ ☐ ☐	Keep a tidy and well-organised unit throughout? ☐ ☐ ☐
Sauté the onions until soft? ☐ ☐ ☐	Prepare, serve and clean within the time available? ☐ ☐ ☐

Q2. Evaluate your dish using the following headings:

COLOUR _____

_____

FLAVOUR _____

_____

TEXTURE _____

_____

CRITICAL FRIEND _____

_____

Q3. Based on your evaluation of the colour, flavour and texture and the comments of your critical friend, identify any changes you would make to your penne al'arrabbiata.

_____

_____

_____

_____

Q4. Boiling and simmering are the cooking methods used in this tomato pasta dish. Explain the difference between these methods.

_____

_____

_____

_____

_____

Q5. Optional activity: Penne al'Arrabbiata is a pasta dish made with a spicy tomato sauce. Examining the ingredients list, identify some modifications you would make to this list to suit the following diets:

Diet	Modifications
Vegan	
Diabetic	
Young child	
Coeliac	

Q6. Optional activity: Pasta is a very popular dish in Ireland. There are many different types and varieties available.

(a) In groups of three–four, choose one/two types of pasta from the box below and research it under the following headings:

○ shape of the pasta (include a picture)

○ examples of popular dishes which include this type of pasta.

Lasagna	Spaghetti	Linguine
Vermicelli	Tagliatelle	Penne
Ravioli	Tortellini	Fettuccine
Macaroni	Rigatoni	Pappardelle

46 Warm Chicken Salad

Serves: 2   **50 mins**

Perfect dish for all class lengths.

Learning Intentions

☆ Demonstrate the correct culinary techniques required to prepare and cook this dish.

☆ Apply appropriate hygiene and safety rules when making this dish.

☆ Evaluate the sensory attributes of this dish and its contribution to a healthy diet.

Ingredients

1 large/2 small skinless chicken breast fillets

⅓ roll black pudding (optional)

1 little gem lettuce

12–14 baby tomatoes

⅓ cucumber

½ yellow/red pepper

3 scallions

10–12 green olives

1 small red onion

50 g cubed Cheddar cheese/blue cheese (for a stronger flavour) (optional)

TO MARINATE THE CHICKEN:

2 tbsp olive oil

2 tbsp balsamic vinegar

salt and freshly ground black pepper

1 tsp fresh rosemary (use dried if fresh is not available)

1 tsp fresh thyme (use dried if fresh is not available)

OPTIONAL MARINADES:

○ lime juice, chilli and honey

○ yogurt and curry powder

○ Cajun spices and olive oil

Equipment

Chopping board(s) (colour-coded), sharp knife, glass bowl, fork/tongs, ovenproof dish, tinfoil, serving bowl, cutlery, two large plates (for cutlery).

Method

1. HANDS, APRON, EQUIPMENT and SET UP UNIT.

2. Preheat the oven 180°C/gas mark 4.

3. Weigh and measure all ingredients.

4. Place the chicken fillets in bowl and pour the olive oil and balsamic vinegar over them.

5. Season with salt, ground black pepper and herbs. Stir/turn the chicken in the marinade using a fork/tongs. Place in an ovenproof dish and cover with tin foil. Bake for 25–30 mins.

6. If using black pudding, cut into small cubes and fry on a dry pan over a medium heat for 5–6 mins.

7. Wash and dry the lettuce, tomatoes, cucumber, pepper and scallions. Cut each baby tomato in half, slice the cucumber. Halve, deseed and slice the pepper into fine strips. Top and tail each scallion and chop into small, even-sized rings. Peel, top, tail and finely slice the red onion.

8. Place all in a serving bowl and gently mix. (This salad can also be served on two individual serving plates.)

9. Remove the chicken from the oven.

10. Using a knife and fork, slice the chicken fillets evenly into long, medium-sized strips.

11. Place the chicken strips and black pudding (if using) on top of the salad. Scatter the olives and cheese on top. Drizzle with balsamic vinegar. Season with black pepper.

TOP TIP

The longer the chicken is marinated in the dressing, the more enhanced the flavours will be. If you can do this a few hours in advance of cooking and leave it covered in the fridge, your dish will be much tastier. There are many different types of marinades to choose from to suit your dish and preferences.

Evaluation

Date of Practical: _____

Q1. Personal Reflection: Did I ...?

Set up my unit correctly? ☐ ☐ ☐

Wash my hands after preparing raw meat? ☐ ☐ ☐

Prepare a tasty marinade that improved the taste of the chicken? ☐ ☐ ☐

Slice vegetables into even slices? ☐ ☐ ☐

Have moist chicken? ☐ ☐ ☐

Slice my chicken evenly for serving? ☐ ☐ ☐

Serve the dish attractively. ☐ ☐ ☐

Have a well-flavoured end product? ☐ ☐ ☐

Keep a tidy and well-organised unit throughout? ☐ ☐ ☐

Prepare, serve and clean within the time available? ☐ ☐ ☐

Q2. Evaluate your dish using the following headings:

COLOUR _____

_____

FLAVOUR _____

_____

TEXTURE _____

_____

CRITICAL FRIEND _____

_____

Q3. Based on your evaluation of the colour, flavour and texture and the comments of your critical friend, identify any changes you would make to your warm chicken salad.

_____

_____

_____

_____

_____

_____

_____

_____

Q4. Identify where you applied specific hygiene and safety rules in the preparation and serving of this dish.

HYGIENE _____

_____

SAFETY _____

_____

Q5. Optional activity: Chicken is low in fat and a very good source of protein. Considering these two factors, name two groups of people you think would nutritionally benefit from including chicken in their diet. Give a reason for each group.

Group of people	Benefit to group

Q6. Optional activity: Give a brief definition of the term 'marinating'. Research the purpose of marinating food. Give examples of three culinary dishes that would benefit from utilising this process.

Definition: _____

Purpose: _____

Dish 1: _____

Dish 2: _____

Dish 3: _____

47 Crispy Smoked Pancetta and Potato Salad

Serves: 4   **50 mins**

For one-hour classes, use pre-cooked potatoes.

Ingredients

500 g baby potatoes (fresh new potatoes are best)

1 tbsp olive oil

170 g diced smoked pancetta

1 small red onion

4 spring onions

2 tbsp mayonnaise (use light mayonnaise for a healthier choice)

salt and pepper

fresh parsley (to garnish)

TOP TIP

For a variation on this dish, add one tablespoon of Dijon mustard. It will give a fresh, zingy taste. This dish is a very good accompaniment to serve at a barbeque. It can be made earlier in the day and refrigerated until required.

Equipment

Chopping board(s) (colour-coded), sharp knife, medium-sized non-stick frying pan, saucepan, tablespoon, mixing bowl, mixing spoon, salad bowl, cutlery, two large plates (for cutlery).

Method

1. HANDS, APRON, EQUIPMENT and SET UP UNIT.

2. Weigh and measure all ingredients.

3. Gently wash and place the potatoes in a pot of salted boiling water for 20 mins or until tender/cooked. Strain and allow to cool before halving.

4. Preheat the non-stick pan on a medium-high setting and add the olive oil.

5. Fry the pancetta until it is a crisp, golden colour (5–10 mins). Stir frequently to avoid burning.

6. Once the pancetta is cooked, remove excess fat by draining on kitchen paper. Allow the pancetta to cool.

7. Peel and finely dice the red onion and spring onions.

8. When the potatoes and pancetta have cooled, place them in the mixing bowl along with the diced red onion and spring onions and fold through the mayonnaise to bind the ingredients.

9. Season with salt and pepper.

10. Serve in a salad bowl and garnish with parsley.

Evaluation

Date of Practical: _____

Q1. Personal Reflection: Did I ...?

Set up my unit correctly? ☐ ☐ ☐

Cook potatoes until tender? ☐ ☐ ☐

Heat oil until hot? ☐ ☐ ☐

Fry the pancetta until it was golden and crisp? ☐ ☐ ☐

Finely dice the red onion and spring onion? ☐ ☐ ☐

Mix the salad until evenly combined? ☐ ☐ ☐

Serve the dish attractively? ☐ ☐ ☐

Have a well-flavoured end product? ☐ ☐ ☐

Keep a tidy and well-organised unit throughout? ☐ ☐ ☐

Prepare, serve and clean within the time available? ☐ ☐ ☐

Q2. Evaluate your dish using the following headings:

COLOUR _____

_____

FLAVOUR _____

_____

TEXTURE _____

_____

CRITICAL FRIEND _____

_____

Q3. Based on your evaluation of the colour, flavour and texture and the comments of your critical friend, identify any changes you would make to your crispy smoked pancetta and potato salad.

_____

_____

_____

_____

_____

_____

_____

Q5. Optional activity: Identify two modifications you could make to the ingredients list to help keep the dish in line with Healthy Eating Guidelines.

Healthy Eating Guideline	Modification
1.	
2.	

Q4. Identify where you applied specific hygiene and safety rules in the preparation and serving of this dish.

HYGIENE _____

_____

_____

_____

SAFETY _____

_____

_____

_____

Q6. Optional activity: Potato is a staple food in Ireland and it can be cooked in many different ways.

(a) Find pictures in a food magazine or online of different ways in which potatoes can be cooked and served. As a class, form a collage of these pictures or form your own individual collage. Display this collage on the Home Economics notice board.

(b) Then as a class, discuss the various ways in which the potatoes have been cooked and in turn how such cooking methods will have affected their nutritive value.

48 Summer Salad with Citrus Dressing

Serves: 4   **45 mins**

This dish is ideal for a one-hour class. Add complexity by grilling some fish or chicken to make this salad a meal.

Ingredients

1 large tomato/8 baby tomatoes

¼ cucumber

½ red onion/4 spring onions

1 avocado

1 mango

50 g feta cheese/goats' cheese/Cheddar cheese etc.

25 g pumpkin/sunflower seeds

½ bag baby spinach leaves

OPTIONAL SALAD EXTRAS:
sweetcorn, radish, chickpeas, beetroot, nuts, sesame/poppy seeds

FOR THE DRESSING:
100 ml olive oil

1 tbsp honey

4 tbsp white wine vinegar

2 limes

OPTIONAL DRESSING EXTRAS:
chopped fresh chilli, fresh mint, fresh basil, fresh coriander, wholegrain mustard

Equipment

Chopping board(s) (colour-coded), sharp knife, juicer, measuring jug, salad bowl, cutlery, two large plates (for cutlery).

Method

1. HANDS, APRON, EQUIPMENT and SET UP UNIT.

2. Wash all salad ingredients that won't be peeled.

3. Remove and discard the wood of the large tomato and slice into narrow wedges/halve the baby tomatoes.

4. Halve the cucumber lengthways and cut into batons. (Cucumber can be peeled but this is not essential.)

5. Peel and thinly slice the red onion/top and tail the spring onion and cut into thin circles.

6. Halve the avocado and remove the stone. Scoop out the flesh with a spoon and slice.

7. Peel and slice the mango into chunks. Alternatively, cut on each side of the stone and make into a 'hedgehog'. Remove these chunks from the skin for the salad.

8. Roughly chop the cheese into 1 cm chunks.

9. Preheat a frying pan on a high heat. Add the chosen seeds to this dry hot pan and cook for 2–3 mins until the seeds are 'popping' and slightly browned. Leave to cool.

10. Wash, dry and place the spinach in the serving bowl. Arrange the rest of the salad ingredients and cheese attractively on top and sprinkle over the cooled seeds.

11. To make the dressing: Add the oil, honey and vinegar to a bowl. Halve and juice the limes. Add the juice to the dressing ingredients and stir well. Serve the dressing on the side.

TOP TIP

Salad dressing will keep in a fridge for a couple of weeks so can be made in bulk. This is a great idea for barbeque season!

TOP TIP

Bags of lettuce spoil faster than bags of spinach. Spinach can be used instead of lettuce in a salad or as a vegetable in many main course dishes. Consider using spinach as an alternative to lettuce as in this recipe, which can help to reduce food waste.

Evaluation

Date of Practical: _____

Q1. Personal Reflection: Did I ...?

Set up my unit correctly? ☐ ☐ ☐

Wash the ingredients as necessary? ☐ ☐ ☐

Chop ingredients evenly? ☐ ☐ ☐

Toast seeds without burning them? ☐ ☐ ☐

Make a tasty salad dressing? ☐ ☐ ☐

Serve the dish attractively. ☐ ☐ ☐

Have a well-flavoured end product? ☐ ☐ ☐

Keep a tidy and well-organised unit throughout? ☐ ☐ ☐

Prepare, serve and clean within the time available? ☐ ☐ ☐

Q2. Evaluate your dish using the following headings:

COLOUR _____

_____

FLAVOUR _____

_____

TEXTURE _____

_____

CRITICAL FRIEND _____

_____

Q3. Based on your evaluation of the colour, flavour and texture and the comments of your critical friend, identify any changes you would make to your summer salad with citrus dressing.

_____

_____

_____

_____

Q4. Identify where you applied specific hygiene and safety rules in the preparation and serving of this dish.

HYGIENE _____

_____

SAFETY _____

_____

Q5. Optional activity: Salads are a valuable source of foods from the fruit and vegetable group. Identify four food combinations you could serve with this salad to make a complete and balanced meal (at least three food groups). The first one is done for you.

Food combinations	Food groups present
Summer salad with baby potatoes and grilled salmon	Fruit and vegetables (salad) Bread and cereal (potato) Meat, fish, alternatives (salmon)

Q6. Optional activity: Spinach leaves were used in this recipe instead of lettuce leaves as they have a longer shelf life after having been picked.

(a) List four fruits/vegetables that are sometimes bought in excess and wasted in your home.

(b) Name a salad that could be made that includes these fruits and vegetables.

Food item	Possible salad
1.	
2.	
3.	
4.	

UNIT 9
Milk, Eggs and Cheese

49. SAVOURY OMELETTE

50. GARLIC MAC AND CHEESE

51. HOMEMADE CHEESY PIZZA

49 Savoury Omelette

Learning Intentions

☆ Choose ingredients to make a healthy dish.

☆ Apply appropriate hygiene and safety rules when making this dish.

☆ Demonstrate the correct culinary techniques required to prepare and cook this dish.

☆ Evaluate the sensory attributes of this dish and its contribution to a healthy diet.

Serves: 1   **15 mins**

Perfect dish for all class lengths.

Ingredients

3 eggs

1 tbsp milk

salt and pepper to taste

30 g grated Cheddar cheese

1 tbsp olive oil/1 tbsp butter

chives/fresh parsley (to garnish)

A variety of food are suitable as fillings for a savoury omelette. With your cooking partner, choose a selection of meat and/or vegetables to make your omelette.

MEAT OPTIONS:

25–30 g smoked pancetta

25–30 g sliced ham

25–30 g cubed bacon

25–30 g diced chorizo

25–30 g smoked salmon

VEGETABLES OPTIONS:

1 spring onion

¼ red/yellow bell pepper

2 mushrooms

2–3 baby tomatoes

½ avocado

Equipment

Chopping board(s) (colour-coded), sharp knife, fork, tablespoon, frying pan, measuring jug, small mixing bowl, spatula, plate to serve, cutlery, two large plates (for cutlery).

Method

1. HANDS, APRON, EQUIPMENT and SET UP UNIT.

2. Weigh and measure all ingredients.

3. In a mixing bowl, gently beat the eggs together with the milk (optional), using a fork. Add salt and pepper to taste.

4. *Optional ingredients:* Dice/cut meat into small cubes/slices. Wash, top and tail the spring onion and chop into fine circles. Wash, deseed and finely slice or dice the pepper. Wash mushrooms, remove stalk, slice and dice. Wash and slice the baby tomatoes. Halve the avocado and remove the stone, scoop out, slice and dice.

5. Heat a medium-sized non-stick frying pan over a medium heat and heat the olive oil/melt the butter. Gently fry your chosen optional ingredients for 3–4 mins, remove from the pan and place in a bowl.

6. Pour the egg mixture into the pan and allow to cook for 10–20 seconds.

7. When you see the egg start to firm up, sprinkle the cheese and optional ingredients on one half of the omelette. Use the spatula to ease the edge of the omelette (with no toppings) and fold this over.

8. Leave to cook for a further minute to melt the cheese.

9. Serve immediately, garnished with the chives/fresh parsley.

TOP TIP

Omelettes are a cheap, quick and nutritious meal to make. For those of you interested in a career as a chef, potential chefs are sometimes asked to demonstrate their skills in making the perfect omelette. It is well worth perfecting your favourite one!

Evaluation

Date of Practical: _____

Q1. Personal Reflection: Did I ...?

Set up my unit correctly? ☐ ☐ ☐

Slice meat evenly? ☐ ☐ ☐

Dice vegetables evenly? ☐ ☐ ☐

Heat oil until hot? ☐ ☐ ☐

Add ingredients in the correct order? ☐ ☐ ☐

Use the right cooking time for the omelette? ☐ ☐ ☐

Use the correct cooking temperature? ☐ ☐ ☐

Roll or fold the omelette to serve? ☐ ☐ ☐

Serve the dish attractively? ☐ ☐ ☐

Have a well-flavoured end product? ☐ ☐ ☐

Keep a tidy and well-organised unit throughout? ☐ ☐ ☐

Prepare, serve and clean within the time available? ☐ ☐ ☐

Q2. Evaluate your dish using the following headings:

COLOUR _____

_____

FLAVOUR _____

_____

TEXTURE _____

_____

CRITICAL FRIEND _____

_____

Q3. Based on your evaluation of the colour, flavour and texture and the comments of your critical friend, identify any changes you would make to your savoury omelette.

_____

_____

_____

_____

_____

_____

Q4. Frying is the cooking method used in this dish. State two safety guidelines to follow when frying food.

Guideline 1:

_____

_____

Guideline 2:

_____

Q5. Optional activity: Use/adapt the ingredients list to help you design a savoury omelette suitable for the following two diets:

Diet	Omelette ingredients
Lacto-vegetarian	
Individual on a weight-loss diet	

Q6. Optional activity: Research the difference between a frittata and an omelette. Identify three benefits of cooking frittatas/omelettes.

Difference between frittata and omelette:

_____

_____

_____

_____

_____

_____

_____

Three benefits:

1. _____

2. _____

3. _____

50 Garlic Mac and Cheese

Learning Intentions

☆ Use a variety of preparation and cooking techniques to make this dish.

☆ Apply appropriate hygiene and safety rules when making this dish.

☆ Demonstrate creative skills in serving this dish attractively.

☆ Evaluate the sensory attributes of this dish and its contribution to a healthy diet.

☆ Compare and evaluate the contribution of commercial roux sauces in the diet.

Serves: 4   45 mins

Perfect dish for all class lengths.

Ingredients

250 g macaroni

40 g butter

40 g plain flour

250 g grated Cheddar cheese + 50 g grated parmesan/300 g any grated cheese

10 cloves garlic

600 ml milk

OPTIONAL INGREDIENTS:

Choose none or just 1 if you have a one-hour class. Choose 2/3 if you have longer.

8 cherry tomatoes

1 pepper

50 g smoked salmon

50 g cold cooked meat

small can sweetcorn

5 rashers/50 g bacon lardons

Equipment

Chopping board(s) (colour-coded), sharp knife, colander, measuring jug, weighing scales, whisk, grater, tin opener, two saucepans, wooden spoon, ovenproof dish, oven gloves, cutlery, two large plates (for cutlery).

Method

1. HANDS, APRON, EQUIPMENT and SET UP UNIT.

2. Preheat the oven to 180°C/gas mark 4.

3. Cook the macaroni in a large saucepan of boiling salted water for 8–10 mins. It will be a little undercooked as it will be cooked further later in the process. Strain well in a colander and set aside.

4. Prepare the optional ingredients: halve the tomatoes. Wash, halve, deseed, slice and dice the pepper. Cut the meat/salmon into thin slices, slice thinly and fry the rashers in a hot frying pan until crisp/fry the bacon lardons in a hot frying pan until crisp.

5. Peel the garlic and slice it thinly.

6. Melt the butter over a medium heat in a saucepan. Add the garlic and cook it gently in the butter for 2 mins. Add the flour and stir to form a roux, cooking for 2 mins.

7. Take the saucepan off the heat and gradually whisk in the milk, a little at a time.

8. Return the saucepan to a medium heat. Bring to the boil, stirring all the time. Turn the heat down and simmer for 2–3 mins until the sauce is thick and smooth.

9. Remove the sauce from the heat, add most of the cheese and stir until it is well combined and melted.

10. Add the macaroni and the optional ingredients to the sauce and mix well. Transfer to an ovenproof dish.

11. Sprinkle over the remaining cheese(s) and place the dish in the oven.

12. Cook for 20 mins until the cheese is browned and bubbling.

13. Remove from the oven using oven gloves and serve hot with a green salad or some steamed broccoli.

TOP TIP

It is crucial when making your roux sauce that you take your time and stir well while adding the milk. A well-made roux sauce is made by a patient chef!

Evaluation

Date of Practical: _____

Q1. Personal Reflection: Did I ...?

Set up my unit correctly? ☐ ☐ ☐

Strain the pasta safely? ☐ ☐ ☐

Prepare optional ingredients before making the roux? ☐ ☐ ☐

Add the milk in small amounts? ☐ ☐ ☐

Make a smooth, thick roux sauce? ☐ ☐ ☐

Cook dish until the cheese bubbled? ☐ ☐ ☐

Serve the dish attractively? ☐ ☐ ☐

Have a well-flavoured end product? ☐ ☐ ☐

Keep a tidy and well-organised unit throughout? ☐ ☐ ☐

Prepare, serve and clean within the time available? ☐ ☐ ☐

Q2. Evaluate your dish using the following headings:

COLOUR _____

_____

FLAVOUR _____

_____

TEXTURE _____

_____

CRITICAL FRIEND _____

_____

Q3. Based on your evaluation of the colour, flavour and texture and the comments of your critical friend, identify any changes you would make to your garlic mac and cheese.

_____

_____

_____

_____

Q4. Define the cooking term 'roux' and list three rules to follow when making a roux sauce.

Definition: _____

_____

_____

Rule 1: _____

Rule 2: _____

Rule 3: _____

Q5. Optional activity: Macaroni cheese is a healthy and nutritious meal. Identify a different nutritional reason why each of the following groups would benefit from this dish.

Group	Nutritional benefit
Convalescent	
Pregnant woman	
Elderly person with osteoporosis	

Q6. Optional activity: Convenience foods play an important role in the lifestyle of a busy family. However, they are often nutritionally inferior to homemade versions.

(a) Make a nutritional comparison between a dried white sauce and a jar of white sauce under the headings given. Make sure you are comparing the foods per 100 g.

Nutrient	Dried sauce	Jar of sauce
Energy (kcal)		
Fat		
Of which saturates		
Carbohydrates		
Of which sugars		
Fibre		
Protein		
Salt		

(b) Evaluate which convenience sauce is the best buy for a busy household. Give two nutritional reasons for your answer.

Chosen sauce: _____

Reason 1: _____

Reason 2: _____

2. STUDENT REFLECTION

Feedback from my teacher:

Feedback from a classmate:

From your feedback, name two aspects of your Food Literacy Skills Brief that are of a high standard:

1. _____

   _____

2. _____

   _____

From your feedback, name two aspects of your Food Literacy Skills Brief that need some further work:

1. _____

   _____

2. _____

   _____

List any changes you would make to your Food Literacy Skills Brief and give reasons why these changes should be made. If you do not need/wish to make changes, please give reasons why this is the case.

Change needed?   Yes ☐   No ☐

(If Yes) State change(s) you should make:

_____

_____

_____

_____

Reasons for change/Reasons for no change being necessary:

1. _____

_____

2. _____

_____

3. _____

_____

4. _____

_____

PART B – PRACTICAL SKILLS EXAM (SAMPLE LAYOUT)

Name of dish:

_____

Ingredients I need:

Equipment I need:

Serving dish:

_____

Preparation time:

_____

What to do during preparation:

1. _____

2. _____

3. _____

4. _____

5. _____

6. _____

7. _____

Method: What to do during the exam:

_____

_____

_____

_____

_____

_____

_____

_____

_____

_____

_____

_____

_____

_____

_____

_____

_____

_____

_____

_____

_____

_____

_____

_____

_____

Notes

Notes